Musée national du Moyen Age

The Cluny Thermae

Musée national du Moyen Age

The Cluny Thermae

Élisabeth Antoine
Conservateur du patrimoine

Xavier Dectot
Conservateur du patrimoine

Julia Fritsch
Conservateur en chef du patrimoine

Viviane Huchard
Conservateur général
Director of the Musée national du Moyen Age – Cluny Thermae

Sophie Lagabrielle
Conservateur en chef du patrimoine

Florence Saragoza
Conservateur du patrimoine

Cover illustration: Saint Mary Magdalene, circa 1490-1500
See pp. 116-117
Right: Facing Harpies circa 1140-1145
See pp. 48-49

49, rue Étienne-Marcel
75001 Paris

ISBN : 2-7118-4643-1
GA 20 4644

Contents

The courtyard
of the Cluny mansion

Viviane Huchard

From the Cluny Museum to the National Museum of the Middle Ages

The *frigidarium* of the Cluny baths

The National Museum of the Middle Ages (Musée national du Moyen Age) is one of the great national museums in which the quality and the rarity of the collections match the interest and singularity of the buildings that house them. At the time it was founded in 1843, the Cluny museum arose from joining two structures entirely different in character and conception—the Gallo-Roman thermal baths and the medieval mansion that once had been the residence of the Order of Cluny abbots in Paris.

The antique thermal baths

The northern baths, known as the "Cluny Thermae", are the most grandiose and well-preserved relics of the Gallo-Roman civilization north of the Loire River. Built in the first century A.D., they were the largest thermal baths in Lutetia and active up until the end of the third century. Raised on the slopes of the hill overlooking the Seine, the northern Thermae were part of the administrative and commercial city. Initially the buildings, which were flanked by shops, annexes, and lodgings, formed a vast quadrilateral edifice measuring no less than 100 by 65 meters. Although partly in ruins, the volume and height of the *frigidarium* and the integrity of its frame, along with the vast dimensions of the underground areas, attest the Roman builders' ambition and daring.

The uninterrupted use of the *frigidarium,* maintained in the eighteenth century as a copper workshop and accurately documented in a painting by Hubert Robert, favored its conservation. The intact groined vault soars to nearly 15 meters. It rests upon carved consoles shaped like the prow of a ship assumed to be the mark of the powerful corporation of Boatmen from the Lutetian city. Its installations—the water ducts, drainage apertures, and pool—are still visible. The wall masonry, made of ashlar that alternates with rows of bricks to form a clamping, was once faced with marble, paint, or mosaic decoration.

In the mid-nineteenth century when the boulevard Saint-Michel was being laid out, the Thermae were cleared and studied by Théodore Vacquer, the city architect and surveyor, with an eye to joining them up with the museum. After World War II, the wide-ranging excavations undertaken by Paul-Marie Duval and Jean Trouvelot brought to light the original plan of the establishment. Further excavations, carried out from 1990 to 1993, revealed an impressive architectural complexity. The base level walls have survived intact, offering a near-complete picture of the evolution of the establishment's use between the first and third centuries A.D.

Inside the museum, the admirably preserved *frigidarium* survives along with adjoining rooms. Outside, the *caldarium* (whose vault collapsed in 1737), one of the *palaestras* (gymnasiums), and another large room have, for the most part, retained their elevations. Heating sources, water mains, ground elements, and the basement plaster testify to the importance of this building.

The Cluny mansion chapel, circa 1490

The Mansion of the Cluny abbots

In the fourteenth century, the powerful abbots of Cluny in Burgundy purchased several houses in a built-up area that faced the recently created University and leaned against the antique Thermae. At the end of the fifteenth century, Jean III de Bourbon (1456-1480) and then Jacques d'Amboise (1485-1510), whose family won fame through artistic munificence, had a new mansion built. Exclusively for private use, the extent and harmony of its appointments refined "flamboyant" décor express the affluence of a nobleman in the late Middle Ages.

The first mansion erected in Paris between a courtyard and a garden, the U-shaped edifice itself consists of a main building extended by two small wings that bound a trapezoidal inner courtyard, limited by a crenelated blind wall. Backed up against the antique Thermae, it is three stories high and covered by a steep slate roof that echoes the carved dormer windows bearing the arms of the Amboise family, "*trois pals alternés d'or et de gueules*". Inside, the house preserves the volumes of the rooms and the circulation behind the façade from the original layout. The building has several spiral staircases; the largest, which projects into the main courtyard inside an elegant hexagonal tower, bears the arms and motto of its builder Jacques d'Amboise. To the west, the south wing gives onto the courtyard by way of a handsome porticoed gallery enhanced with cales and animals, and on the first floor by way of a covered walk intended to lead to the "wonder" of the place: a hanging garden created over the vaults of the *frigidarium* that the abbots had the right to use. On the north facade, extended by a garden that has now been restored, another wing contains the chapel. Its elaborate feathered arch is an outstanding example of flamboyant gothic architecture at its quintessence. The chapel is enlarged by an elegant oriel containing the altar and adorned with windows originally in stained glass. A staircase with open-work leads to the sunken room giving onto the garden. Its groined vaults

Christ bearing the Cross
stained-glass from
the Cluny mansion,
Paris, circa 1500

The Garden of Love, created by E. Ossart and A Maurière, 2000

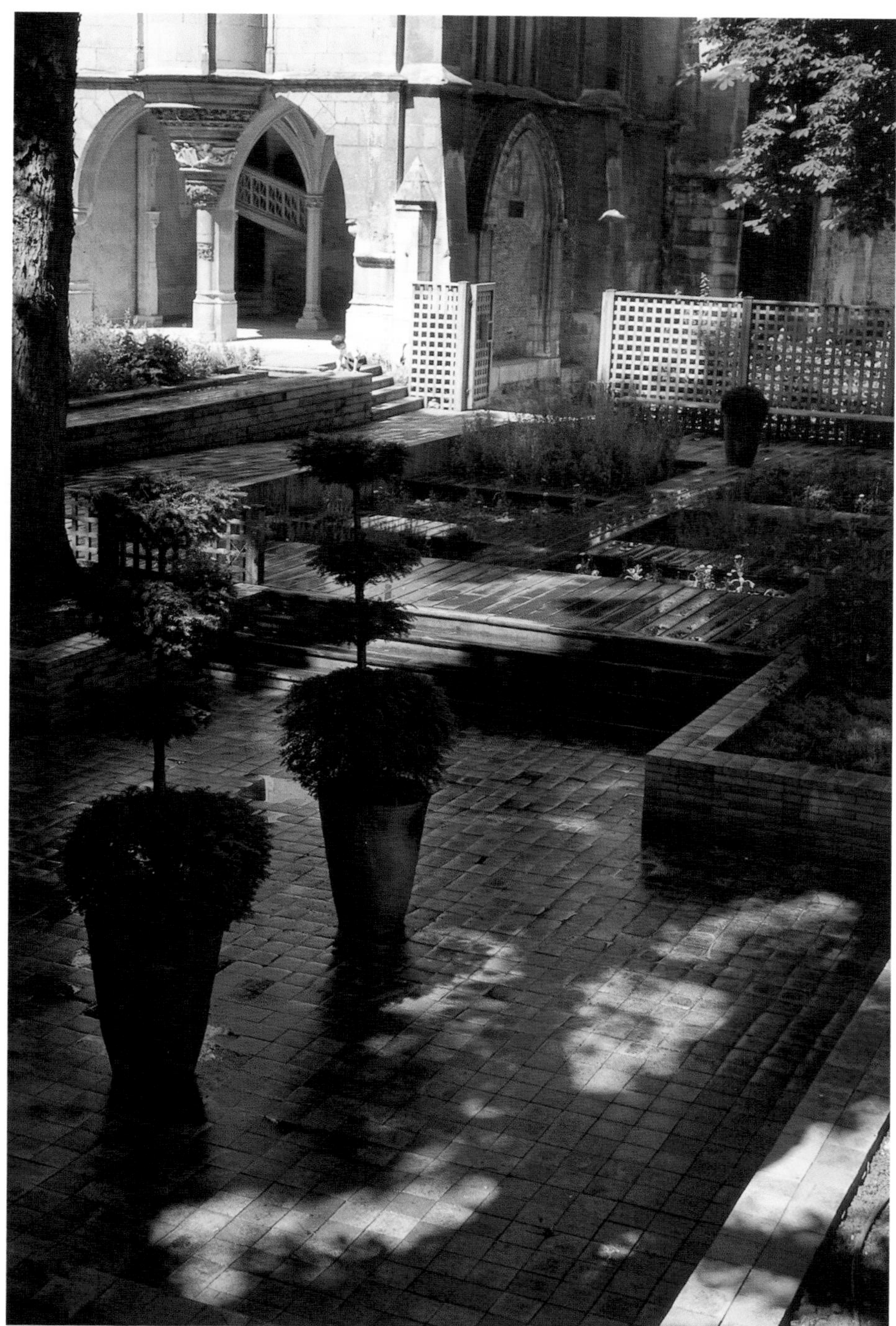

rest upon a central pillar crowned by a capital decorated with leaf-work, and its vase bears the crowned K, the emblem of the French king ruling at the time, Charles VIII (1483-1498).

Residence of the abbots until the sixteenth century, and thereafter of notable guests, the mansion itself was sold during the Revolution as national property, but then suffered alterations and damage before it was acquired by the State in 1843. The architect Albert Lenoir, son of the founder of the Musée des monuments français, then undertook to consolidate the roofs and apertures, rebuild the balustrade, and restore a number of the scuptures on the gable windows. Yet the mansion's overall appearance was preserved, particularly in the main courtyard. The subsequent clearing of the buildings connected with Prefect Haussmann's urbanization projects that insured better visibility of the museum, unfortunately tore down the convent of the Mathurins east of the block in 1869. On the north side, an ample garden planted with trees and enhanced by sculptures separated the museum from the boulevard Saint-Germain.

After the Second World War, while the City of Paris arranged a public square on the remaining area, the private garden of the museum was reduced to a stone yard in front of the mansion. The museum's latest development, in September 2000, was the creation of a medieval-style garden. Now, a large terrace bordered by wooden trellises reaches the boulevard Saint-Germain, opening the museum onto the city. It is laid out in four closed squares, each illustrating one aspect of a Medieval garden. The *Household* or *Kitchen Garden* presents edible plants and vegtables; it grows leeks, Swiss chard, cabbages, parsnip and herbs or a variety of aromatic plants (sorrel, basil and parsley), along with "small fruit" (black currants, currants, physalis). The *Medicinal Herb Garden* is devoted to medicinal plants such as sage, mint, hyssop, rue, melissa, which are grown next to marigolds and chamomile. The *Heavenly Garden* celebrates the Virgin and grows plants and flowers consecrated to Her: violets, lilies, irises, and, of course, roses, the flower of paradise *par excellence*. The *Garden of Love* faithfully reproduces the enclosed spaces illustrated in miniatures. On benches amidst the turf and wafting sweet scents, visitors may let their senses be charmed like the courtly lovers of medieval literature. On the upper terrace, the garden ends in a meadow surrounded by water sewn with the "millefleurs" identified in the museum tapestries, and contains a splashing fountain. These gardens, which are the only ones directly inspired by medieval architecture and a collection of artifacts, have a unique character. The patronage of M. David-Weill made their realization possible, as did the support of the Minister of Culture, and our partners: the Caisse des Dépôts, the City of Paris, Alcatel, Sophia, and the Friends of the Museum.

The Collections

In 1843, the purchase by the French State of Alexandre Du Sommerard's collections and the Cluny mansion containing them, and successively the donation by the City of Paris of the Gallo-Roman Thermae, where various antique and medieval sculptures were kept, mark the birth of the museum. Its mission arises from this original dual nature.

Alexandre Du Sommerard was one of the most colorful among the zealous art lovers of the Romantic era. Born in 1779, his fondness for antiques may have been brought about by his stay in Italy during Napoleon I's campaigns. Later he had an honorable career at the Audit office, and was appointed chief-counselor in 1831. Good-natured and curious, Du Sommerard was sociable and frequently met with artists and men of letters; he also took part in the activities of historical societies engaged in the protection of the monuments and archives of the nation's history.

Alexandre Du Sommerard
Lithograph by
Adolph Godard after
Achille Devéria,
circa 1835

True to the memory of the Musée des monuments français created by Alexandre Lenoir in the convent of the Petits Augustins in the wake of the Revolution, a number of collectors formed curiosities cabinets, among them Carrand, Debruge-Duménil, Révoil, Sauvageot, Willemin, and Denon. Du Sommerard also began to collect artifacts that he would install, in 1832, in the part of the Cluny mansion that a printer had rented him. On half of the first floor, where the chapel lies, the connoisseur stored and exhibited his growing collection. "He did the honors of the house with an exquisite manner, and without appearing to teach, gave lessons in practical archeology that stirred interest and were not forgotten...", Prosper Mérimée wrote. The painter Achille Devéria portrayed the collector holding a Renaissance statuette in his celebrated portrait gallery of contemporaries. At the heart of his mansion, in a stunning setting, he evoked the shades of great men. King François I was particularly glorified; in a room devoted to him, we see his bed, stirrups, and other attributed objects. The collector took advantage of the chapel being on two stories to separate the religious artifacts from the profane. Elsewhere, eras and techniques merged. The most incongruous items, whether modest or precious, are a jumbled assortment regardless of their chronology. We owe to Alexandre Du Sommerard's sagacity the acquisition of remarkable ivories, such as the *Crowning of Otto II and of Theophano*, the Embriachi altarpiece from the Carthusian monastery in Champmol, and mirror frames, as well as the finest Limoges enamels, especially the plaques from the abbey of Grandmont. The books he wrote help us grasp his psychology and the scope of his knowledge. He was a forerunner, publishing his *Les Arts au Moyen Age* in 1840 (later completed by his son Edmond), and extensively illustrating the volume with lithographs of pieces from his own collection as well as from those of his confrères.

At the famous collector's death in 1842, his contemporaries, sensitive to the harmony created between the collection and the monument housing it, wished to make this bond permanent by founding a museum. The process was already under way in 1836, when the City of Paris installed its lapidary deposit, which consisted of sculptures taken from demolitions and restorations of Parisian monuments as well as those from excavations, in the Thermae *frigidarium*. This decision preserved statues from Notre-Dame de Paris and the excavations of Saint-Marcel, as well as several others from the restorations of Saint-Germain-des-Prés. In July 1843, a law sanctioned the creation of a "museum specially devoted to the monuments, furnishings and artifacts of Antiquity, the Middle Ages and the Renaissance". The City yielded to the State the Thermae and the lapidary collections and, in turn, the State bought the mansion and Alexandre Du Sommerard's cabinet. For a long time, together these two ensembles would give this remarkably varied museum its particular character. The educational value of the new establishment was also underscored. The point was to "assemble all the material documents necessary for the history of the Fine Arts in France to give access to artists, men of letters and workmen a reservoir of worthwhile models for archeological studies and the perfecting of industry".

Albert Lenoir had presented his design for a "Historical Museum formed by joining the Thermae and the Cluny mansion" in 1833 at the annual Salon. So once the Cluny and Thermae Museum was formally ratified, he was naturally the one engaged to restore the mansion and establish it as a museum in close cooperation with its director. The buildings were put on the State historical register: the mansion in 1856 and the Thermae in 1862. In September 1843, Edmond Du Sommerard, the collector's son, was appointed curator. As soon as it opened, in March 1844, the museum met with considerable success. The curator's forty-years' administration was to be particularly beneficial, as his long tenure only increased

The room
of king François I,
Lithograph from
A. Du Sommerard,
Les Arts au Moyen Age,
Paris 1840

public loyalty. When Edmond died in 1885, the collections had increased tenfold; though the intimate atmosphere Alexandre Du Sommerard created in the mansion was somewhat compromised. A new building, a pastiche of Roman ruins built on the west façade, held the recent and monumental acquisitions, such as the tapestries and the large Renaissance enamel plaques. The visit included the gardens, enhanced by monumental sculptures and plaster casts. Thanks to his dedication and his rapport with the Historical Monuments commission in charge of the museum at the time, Edmond Du Sommerard attracted countless masterpieces, including the stained-glass windows and the *Apostles* from the Sainte-Chapelle in Paris, the tapestries of *La Vie Seigneuriale* (The Lord's Life), the famous wall-hanging of the *Lady with the Unicorn*, and the equally famous tapestry of *David and Bathsheba* (presently at the Musée de la Renaissance, château d'Écouen). He also enriched the museum with several unique artifacts of goldsmith work by acquiring precious items from the treasury of the Basel cathedral (1854), and the gold crowns of the Visigoth kings (1859). The prestige of the

Hall of sculptures
from Notre-Dame de Paris

museum was such that a number of establishments were created in its likeness; among these are the Bayerisches Museum in Munich and the Schnütgen Museum in Cologne.

Up to World War II, the museum, which continued to increase its collections in the various departments, remained true to its original mission by broadly illustrating the development of the decorative arts from the Middle Ages to the nineteenth century. Its holdings in tapestry, precious fabric, enamel, and furniture gave it a place of honor among French museums. When it reopened in 1946, it entered a new phase. Major architectural interventions were undertaken, while the museum's curators reorganized the display of the works of art. The sculptures of antique Lutetia and the Pillar of the Nautes, along with the Saint-Landry column, were placed in the Thermae *frigidarium*. Artifacts and historical pieces were put on exhibit in the mansion rooms. The collections were presented in keeping with the techniques described in the *Livre des Métiers* (Book of Crafts), written during the reign of King Saint Louis. This museographic selection would lead several years later to the creation of a new museum devoted to the Renaissance at Écouen (1977). Other museums and châteaus, especially those in the provinces, were also able to enrich their ensembles by deposits. In spite of the fact that this manner of presentation gradually became less pertinent, the collections continued to grow. The chance discovery in 1977 of the twenty-one heads of the Kings of Judah from the façade of Notre-Dame de Paris, for instance, represents the most important archeological find of the late 20th century. Their entry into the museum was a spectacular event.

The mission of the monument was once again confirmed in 1992, when it was given the name: "National Museum of the Middle Ages". Consisting of works of art—sculpture, goldsmith work, paintings, tapestries—and items from everyday life—ironworks, pottery, pilgrimage badges, furniture—the collection's more than 20,000 items illustrate every aspect of social and creative life from the end of Antiquity to the dawn of the Renaissance. Originating for the most part in the Christian medieval West—or *Christianitas*—the collections provide an illustration of the geographic and sociological reality of today's Europe. They also allow us to recall on a smaller scale Europe's former neighbors, the Byzantine Empire and the Islamic world. The Gallo-Roman collection related to the history of Paris is appropriately housed in the Thermae *frigidarium*, the largest room Antiquity bequeathed us.

Today, the museum again asserts its identity. It has set out to enliven our perception of the Middle Ages through an ambitious scientific and cultural project backed by the Friends of the Museum and sheperded by the Direction des Musées de France. The main lines of this project preserve and valorize the buildings, and rearrange the collections to make them more legible, while at the same time they integrate the contributions of contemporary museography supported by a national and international scientific network. The project also improves access to the site for an ever-growing and curious public.

From Antiquity to the First Millennium

Traditional history has the Middle Ages begin in 476, the year of the fall of the Western Roman Empire. This long period extends from late Antiquity to the Empire of Otto the Great, from the Barbarian realms to the Carolingian Empire, encompassing interactions among the Byzantine world, Islam, and the Barbarian kingdoms. From the Celtic world, before the Roman conquest, the museum keeps several pieces of goldsmith work that display the Gallic craftsmen's inventive spirit. The *Pax romana* from the first to the third century A.D. brought prosperity and development. Lutetia momentarily became a capital. The Ile de la Cité was the seat of political and religious power, of which

Pillar of Saint-Landry:
Gaule (discovered on the Île de Cité in Paris)
Second half of the IInd century
Stone
Cl.18606

the museum possesses such outstanding vestiges as the pillar of the Nautes and the pillar of Saint-Landry on which Roman and Celtic divinities appear next to one another. At the end of the fourth century, Christianity was pronounced the official religion, but Rome was no longer the capital of the Empire. The Barbarian raids in the third and fourth centuries became Germanic migrations, and the new conquerors—the Visigoths in Spain and the Salians in the Ile-de-France— shared the remains of the Empire. The Western world's dream of unity was fulfilled in 800 by Charlemagne (who was crowned emperor in Rome), before being taken over by a Germanic dynasty, the Ottonians. The exceptional altar front commissioned by emperor Henry II expresses both in the choice of its materials as well as through its iconography, the ambition and wealth of religious foundations. The importance of their role is also reflected in other artistic centers, such as the workshop in Echternach (Lotharingia, present-day Luxembourg) that produced this powerful ivory of Saint Paul.

In the East, the Byzantine Empire, which lasted until the Turks seized Constantinople in 1453, was also subjected to upheavals and influences. Ivories, gemstones, and fabrics brought to the West left their imprint on European productions.

If the center of gravity of the West hinged toward France and Germany, the Empire had to take its neighbors into consideration, in particular those of the Anglo-Saxon world. This new contribution, which clashed with Carolingian and Ottonian classicism, gave rise to Romanesque art that flourished at the dawn of the new millennium.

V. H.

Reliquery plaque: Saint Paul
Echternach
Second quarter of the XIth century
Ivory
Cl. 1505

Treasure of Saint-Marc-le-Blanc

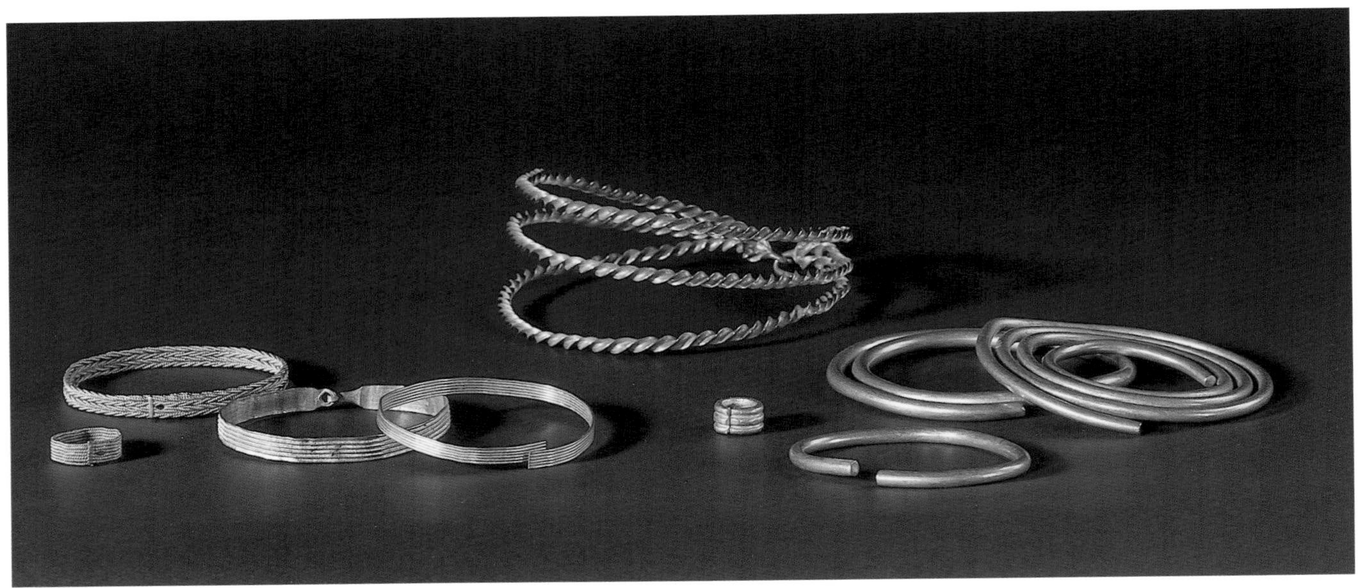

Gold
Weight 479.9 grams
Discovered at Saint-Marc-le-Blanc (Ile-et-Vilaine) in 1854; acquired 1856
Cl. 2629 to Cl. 2637

In 1854, a farmer found a Celtic treasure in his fields consisting of nineteen gold artifacts. At the time of their burial, several pieces had been placed in vases that were eventually lost. Only nine of these are on display in the museum today; the other fragments were probably sold as raw material. The Saint-Marc-le-Blanc treasure is rather heterogeneous in typology (complete jewels, fragments and lingots) and chronology of the works. In fact, the form and high copper content of the smooth bracelet and the composite ring suggest they belong to the goldsmithwork of the late Bronze Age (1200-800 B.C.). The other artifacts form a group that may have been assembled in the sixth century B.C. Notice, for example, the prevalence of a decoration based on coiled filigree in the jewelry. Their craftmanship is similar to artifacts from the Castros culture (Spain) dated to the Iron Age.

F. S.

Pillar of the Nautes

Stone (Lutetian limestone from Saint-Leu-d'Esserent, Oise)
H. 1.10 m; W. 0.75 m
H. 0.47 m; W. 0.74 m
H. 0.47 m; W. 0.74 m
H. 0.45 m; W. 0.91 m
Discovered on the Ile-de-la-Cité in Paris; assigned to the museum in 1844
Cl. 18602 to Cl. 18605

The Pillar of the Nautes is the oldest dated Paris monument. Indeed, the Latin dedication confirms that it was raised under Tiberius' consulate (14-37 A.D.). The five stones discovered under the chancel of Notre-Dame cathedral during eighteenth-century alterations were originally put one on top of another to form a pillar dedicated to the god Jupiter. Unlike other known pillars, the one in the museum, the oldest, associates Celtic with Roman pantheons. The Latin and Gallic inscriptions above the representations of the divinities identify the gods of each community -Jupiter, Vulcan, the Dioscures, along with Esus, Cernunnos, Tarvos Trigaranus. This monument is evidence of Rome's capacity to assimilate other cultures. The pillar was commissioned and sponsored by the Boatmen's corporation in charge of the river trade on the Seine and its tributaries, but unfortunately its site in ancient Lutetia is unknown.

F. S.

Statue known as "Julian the Apostate"

Naxos marble
H. 1.80 m
Millioti collection, Dumont collection; La Riboisière collection, purchased in 1859
Cl. 18830

This work was purchased toward the middle of the nineteenth century when the Cluny Thermae were being cleared and consolidated. At that time, they were believed to be the ruins of the palace of the emperor Julian the Apostate (360-363 A.D.). The count La Riboisière sold the sculpture to the museum, claiming it had been discovered in Paris. In fact, the statue, as well as a similar one presently in the Louvre, was brought from Italy by an Italian-born antique dealer, Alphonse D. Gaspard Milliotti. The attribution was also erroneous; the work actually represents a priest, identified by the diadem the figure wears. His features, the rendering of his hair and beard, along with the composition of the drapery, connect this piece to the age of Hadrian, that is, to the second century A.D.

F. S.

IVth-VIth century A.D.(?)

Rock crystal Lion Heads

Rock crystal
H. 0.125 m; W. 0.09 m;
D. 0.10 m;
H. 0.12 m; W. 0.083 m;
D. 0.095 m
Du Sommerard Collection
Cl. 615 and Cl. 616

The two identical heads are most likely a pair that was once attached to a piece of furniture; they are hollow and have a groove in their lower part to affix them. The two lions are represented with their mouths open. An aperture was made level with the corners of the lips so that a separate element, perhaps a ring, could be slipped inside. Convincing comparisons with coins and ivory consular diptychs closely associate these works with the ornaments of an imperial or consular throne. Yet the lack of any real parallel with similar work makes it difficult to locate and date the heads. Nonetheless, the material itself as well as the symbolism connected with lions links these pieces to late Antique imperial circles.

F. S.

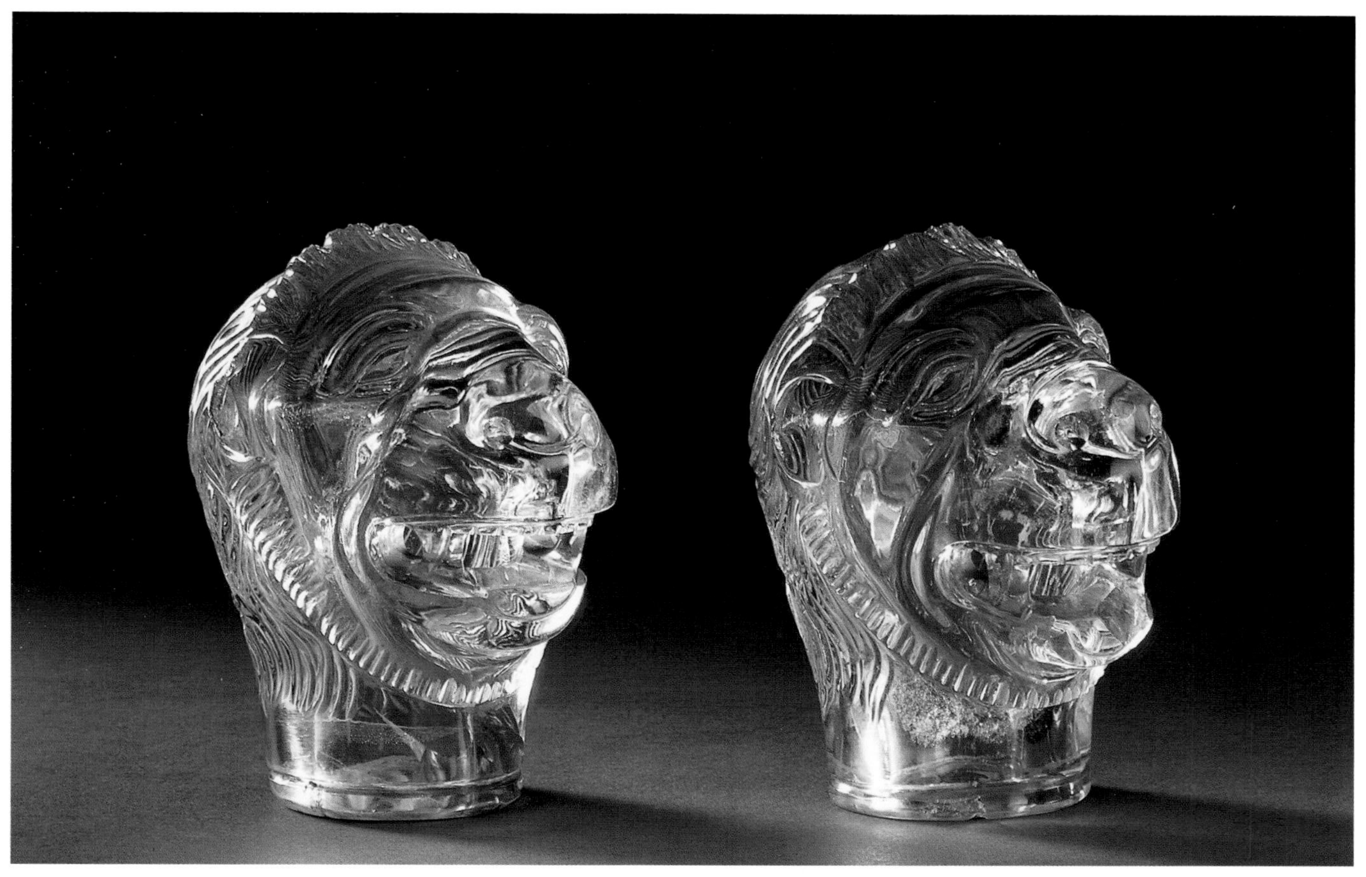

Vth century A.D.

Appliqué group: Ariadne, maenad, satyr and cupids

Bracket group
Elephant ivory formerly inlaid
H. 0.40 m; W. 0.138 m; D. 0.0075 m
Du Sommerard collection
Cl. 445

This group in very high relief is composed around the representation of a young woman, leaning against the trunk of a knotty tree. Her right arm rests on a thyrse topped by a bouquet of ivy leaves. The incisions made at its bottom suggest that the cup she is holding is full. Her face is perfectly oval. The drooping eyes under heavy eyelids were formerly inlaid with glass beads. The nose protrudes over a small mouth. The face is framed in wavy locks of hair parted in the middle that fall over her shoulders. The young woman is wearing a long *chiton* baring her right breast, a cloak drawn up over her head, and sandals with two thongs. She is flanked by two figures: to her left a dancing satyr, to her right a maenad holding a pair of cymbals. They are the traditional participants in bacchic processions. Crowning the composition, two cupids raise a crown that confirms the identity of the female figure. The presence of the satyr and the maenad associate her with the *thiase* of Dionysus. But the crown argues for the god's mate, Ariadne. It was, in fact, Ariadne who became Dionysus' symbol in the *Corona Borealis* constellation.

When it was acquired, this ivory was said to have been discovered with the two lion heads described in the preceding notice, "in a grave by the Rhine River". However, the good state of conservation suggests that this work had never been buried.

The date and provenance of the work were initially based on a comparison with the leaf of an imperial diptych kept in the Bargello Museum of Florence that depicts the empress Ariadne, wife of Anastasius (491-518 A.D.). That ivory, from the imperial workshops, is dated to the early sixth century. The high relief and delicacy of the museum's example also leads one to think of productions from imperial circles, such as the Barberini ivory in the Louvre that probably depicts the emperor Justinian (527-565).

Iconographically, the museum's bracket is similar to late Antique ivories that were reutilized in emperor Henry II's ambo in Aachen, and attributed to Alexandrian workshops. We can, therefore, posit a Near-Eastern origin and a sixth-century date for the museum's Ariadne. And yet, the style of the piece is very different. For example, the ivory representing Ariadne is characterized by its imitation of classical models, which leads us to think it may emulate a specific antique work.

The Ariadne relief has another aspect in common with Alexandrian ivories: its curved shape. The artifact's large dimensions as well as its attachment holes suggest this object may have once belonged to a piece of furniture. Another piece, adorned with the figure of Dionysus, might well have been the pendant of this bracket group.

F. S.

E G Y P T

Vth-VIth century A.D.

Jason and Medea

Linen and wool
Tapestry, paired warp threads
Diam. 0.07 m
Probably discovered at Antinoöpolis; Côte bequest 1961
Cl. 22813

Originally, this medallion probably adorned a tunic, a garment worn in the Coptic period by men as well as women. A line of undyed scrolls bordered by a single fillet ending in a vine leaf forms the trimming of the *orbiculus* on a plain dark purple ground. In the middle, a scene with two figures represents the central episode of the myth of the Golden Fleece. Medea, on the left and in profile, distracts the serpent appointed to watch over the Fleece with her bowl. The latter is shown at the top of a tree that also marks the vertical axis of the composition. On the right, Jason is depicted naked, grasping the precious treasure.

This iconography is rarely found on antique textiles. Its presence suggests a literary intention. The medallion itself is related to a group of tapestry *orbiculi* on a purple ground with scroll trimmings, some of which are kept in the Louvre in Paris, the Musée départemental des Antiquités in Rouen, the Musée des Beaux-Arts in Dijon, the Georges-Labit museum in Toulouse, and the Museums of Fine Arts in Boston and Saint Petersburg. They are dated between the fifth and sixth centuries A.D.

F. S.

C O N S T A N T I N O P L E

506 A.D.

Panel from the diptych of the consul Areobindus

Elephant ivory adorned with inlays now lost
H. 0.39 m; W. 0.13 m
Inscription: *Former count of the sacred stable* [of the imperial stables] *and master of the soldiers for the Orient, former consul, ordinary consul*
De La Mare collection;
Du Tillot Collection;
De Ruffey collection;
Vesvrottes collection;
Baudot collection;
acquired 1894
Cl. 13135

Consular diptychs are gifts the consul sent when he assumed his charge to those who had supported his candidacy.

The position of the hinges indicates that this piece was the lower section of a diptych. Only the outer side was decorated; the inner side was hollowed and filled with wax and used as a writing tablet. The iconography

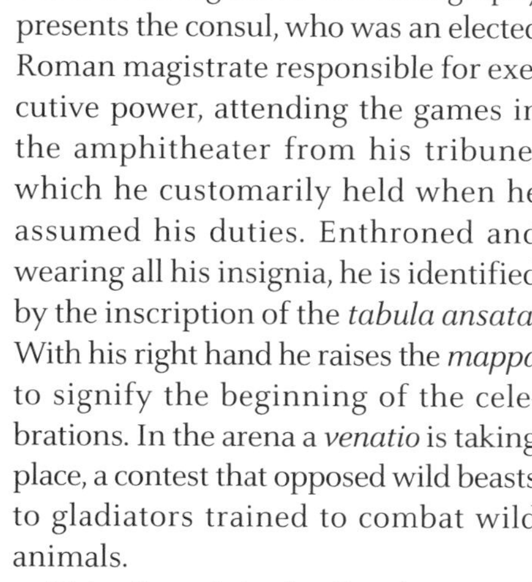

presents the consul, who was an elected Roman magistrate responsible for executive power, attending the games in the amphitheater from his tribune, which he customarily held when he assumed his duties. Enthroned and wearing all his insignia, he is identified by the inscription of the *tabula ansata*. With his right hand he raises the *mappa* to signify the beginning of the celebrations. In the arena a *venatio* is taking place, a contest that opposed wild beasts to gladiators trained to combat wild animals.

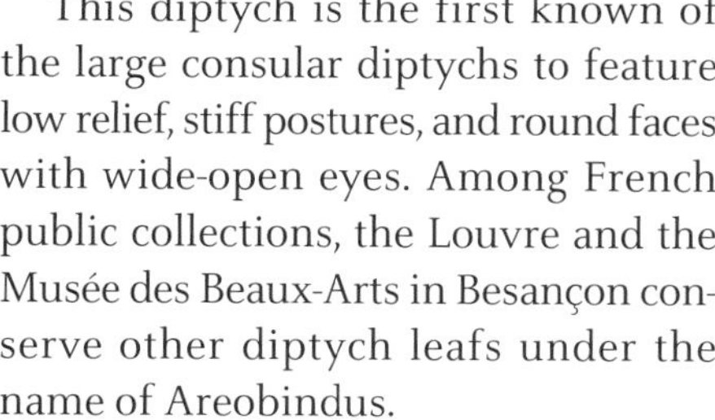

This diptych is the first known of the large consular diptychs to feature low relief, stiff postures, and round faces with wide-open eyes. Among French public collections, the Louvre and the Musée des Beaux-Arts in Besançon conserve other diptych leafs under the name of Areobindus.

F. S.

Treasure of Guarrazar

Votive crown with cross
Gold, sapphire, emeralds, pearls, quartz, amethysts, glass beads
H. 0.673 m; maximum Diam. 0.168 m
Acquired 1859
Cl. 2879

Votive crown
Gold, sapphire, emeralds, pearls, amethysts, glass beads
H.0.47 m; Diam. 0.13 m
Acquired 1861
Cl. 3211

Votive crown
Gold, glass beads
H. 0.17 m; Diam. 0.11 m
Acquired 1859
Cl. 2885

Votive cross
Gold, sapphire, pearls, amethysts, jasper
H. 0.185 m; W. 0.108 m
Acquired 1859
Cl. 2880

Letter pendant of the votive crown of Receswinthe
Gold, sapphire, pearl, garnet, glass beads
H. 0.084 m; maximum Diam. 0.023 m
Acquired 1859
Cl. 2878

Suspension parts of a votive crown
Gold
H. 0.102 m; W. 0.028 m; Diam. 0.002 m
Acquired1859
Cl. 23215 a and b

Suspension parts of a votive crown
Gold
H. 0.51 m and H. 0.206 m
Acquired 1859
Cl. 23216 a and b

Pendant of a votive crown
Gold, pearl, glass beads
H. 0.046 m
Acquired1859
Cl. 23217

Pendant of a votive crown
Gold, sapphire
H. 0.019 m
Acquired 1859
Cl. 23218

Ensemble found at Guarrazar, near Toledo (Spain)

Sometime between 1858 and 1860, a retired French officer residing near Toledo in the locality of La Fuente de Guarrazar undertook excavations on his property. In all, he found twenty-six crowns. Fourteen were melted down at the Mint in Madrid and turned into lingots; France acquired eight for the Cluny museum. Of the remaining four, one was acquired by the museum and the three others, offered to Isabel II of Spain, were deposited at the Real Armería of Madrid, where two of them were stolen in 1921. Six of the nine Cluny crowns were part of a "trade", ratified by the law of July 19, 1941, between the government of the Maréchal Pétain, former French ambassador to Franco, and the Spanish government. The trade also included the Lady of Elche, a masterpiece of Iberic sculpture, and the *Soult Immacolata* by Murillo, henceforth exhibited at the Museo Arqueólogico Nacional in Madrid.

The offering of votive crowns that faithfully emulate the symbol of royal power is a Byzantine practice traced to Constantinople by the sixth century but one that seems to go back to Constantine himself. It appears

again by 587 in the Iberic peninsula, and, according to a slightly later chronicle, Reccared, the first Visigoth sovereign to reject Arianism for Catholicism, placed one over the tomb of Felix, martyr of Gerona. The custom became widespread once the Visigothic *Liber ordinum* passed down the text of a blessing specially conceived for such ceremonies. We should note that though such offerings may have been performed by sovereigns, as suggested by the crown offered by Receswinthe (from which the museum conserves a letter pendant Cl. 2878), this was not always the case. The crown Cl. 2879 bears a votive cross indicating it was offered by someone named Sonnica, a name no Visigoth king in Spain ever bore.

The museum's crowns, buried in 711 when the Berber-Arab troops of Tarik ben-Zyad invaded the peninsula, present three different types: Sonnica's is formed with a full band, a second is trellis-shaped, the third is perforated in arcades. They come from the churches of Toledo, capital of the kingdom, and demonstrate the richness of the goldsmithwork that adorned these edifices documented by both Christian and Islamic chronicles.

X. D.

Quadriga

Figured samite, polychrome silks
H. 0.75 m; W. 0.725 m
Treasury of the cathedral of Aachen; de Vielcastel collection; donation to the Louvre in 1850; deposited in the museum in 1895
Cl. 13289

The decor, yellow on a blue ground, is inscribed in large medallions trimmed with a crown adorned with lotus buds. The main scene shows a charioteer holding the reins of a quadriga. Beside him, the small figures that either offer a crown and a whip or emptying bags of coins identify him as the winner of the race. The costumes—short tunics, *chlamys* and laced boots—like the horses' saddlery, recall ivory consular diptychs. This image of victory in the circus is related to the imperial triumph cycle and can be found in other silks. According to tradition, this piece of cloth would have been used to wrap the body of Charlemagne, who was buried in Aachen, his capital.

V. H.

The Crowning of Otto II and Theophano

Binding plaque
Elephant ivory
H. 0.18 m; W. 0.10 m;
D. 0.008 m
Inscriptions: *Otto, Emperor of the Romans, August / Theophano, Empress, August / Lord, assist your servant John...*
Du Sommerard collection
Cl. 392

The two rivet holes that survive in the upper part of the plaque indicate this ivory once enhanced a binding board. The scene unfolds inside the field bound by a continuous lintel. Under a canopy, Christ places twin crowns upon the heads of two smaller figures. They are identified by inscriptions that state their names and titles in a mix of Latin and Greek. The Emperor Otto II and his wife Theophano of Constantinople extend their right hands toward Christ in a gesture of veneration. Their attire and crowns, as well as the overall scheme of the work awkwardly emulate models in use in the Byzantine Empire. In fact, the work has been compared to the plaque of the emperor Roman II's crowning conserved in the Cabinet des Médailles at the Bibliothèque Nationale in Paris. Thus the museum's ivory shows the influence exerted by Byzantium on the European courts at that time. A fourth figure, prostrated before Christ, appears at the sovereign's feet. An invocation to Christ, this figure of John is incised along the column. For some scholars, he might be the bishop John Philagathos, who contributed to the reconciliation with the Byzantine Empire. The title borne by the sovereign suggests the work dates to 982-983 A.D., the year of Otto II's death. It offers stylistic similarities with the ivory group known as "Nicephore", but appears to have been crafted in a Western workshop.

F. S.

Portable altar

Porphyry and gilded silver on wooden core
H. 0.256 m; W. 0.23 m
Inscription: *Here are deposited relics of Saint John the Baptist and the martyrs Cyriacus, Pancras, Kilian*
Londesborough Collection; Spitzer collection; acquired 1893
Cl. 13072

This piece of goldsmithwork frames a plaque of antique green porphyry that is inserted in a wooden core faced with gilded silver leaf and adorned with etchings. It is a portable altar, housing relics of the Saints John the Baptist, Cyriacus, Pancras, and Kilian, as attested to by the inscription engraved on the edge of the object. It enabled clerics and prelates to celebrate mass during their travels.

The decoration is bordered by bands of ornamental plants. In the upper register the beardless Christ appears in a mandorla. He holds out the keys to Saint Peter and offers the Book to Saint Paul, in keeping with the *traditio legis et clavum* design. Saint Blaise and Saint Nicholas appear in the corners. In the lower part, three Old Testament figures – Melchisedech presenting the paten and the chalice, Aaron holding an incensor, and Abraham about to sacrifice his son – announce the sacrament of the Eucharist. On the back, the decoration is inscribed in five medallions on a foliated scroll. We can identify the divine Lamb and the four cardinal virtues. The iconography of the artifact itself is associated with the celebration of mass.

This alter recalls countless goldsmithworks produced under the rule of the emperor Henry II (1002-1024) inspired by the *scriptoria* of Fulda, but was probably crafted at Bamberg.

F. S.

FULDA OU BAMBERG (?)

XIth Century

Altar front from Basel cathedral

Gold on oak core, wax stuffing, gilded and enamelled copper, gilded silver and copper alloy, pearls, silver balls, glass beads, precious and semi-precious stones
H. 1.20 m; W. 1.775 m; D. 0.13 m
Inscription: *Who [is], like God strong, a doctor and a saviour? Benedict*
Treasury of the Basel cathedral; Handmann collection; Theubet collection; acquired 1854

This rectangular work is circumscribed by an ornamental frame with vegetal decoration. Five semi-circular arcades supported by columns occupy the main field. In each of the intercolumniations a figure standing on a hillock points at a Latin inscription. In the middle, Christ is represented full front, blessing and displaying the orb stamped with His monogram. The two crowned figures bowed down at his feet are identified in medieval tradition as the Ottonian sovereign Henry II and his wife Cunegunda. To the left, the archangel Michael holds the orb and standard; Saint Benedict, who is shown with the crozier and a book, flanks him. Archangels Gabriel and Raphael appear on the right. Above the arcades a vegetal decoration unfolds, interrupted by four medallions featuring the cardinal virtues. This iconographic program not only glorifies the power of Christ but also that of his representative on Earth, the emperor.

The complicated inscription on the altar tablet seems to designate the Benedictine convent of Michelsberg in Bamberg as the original destination of the *antependium*. However, Henri II first offered it to the Basel cathedral on the occasion of one of his sojourns in the city.

F. S.

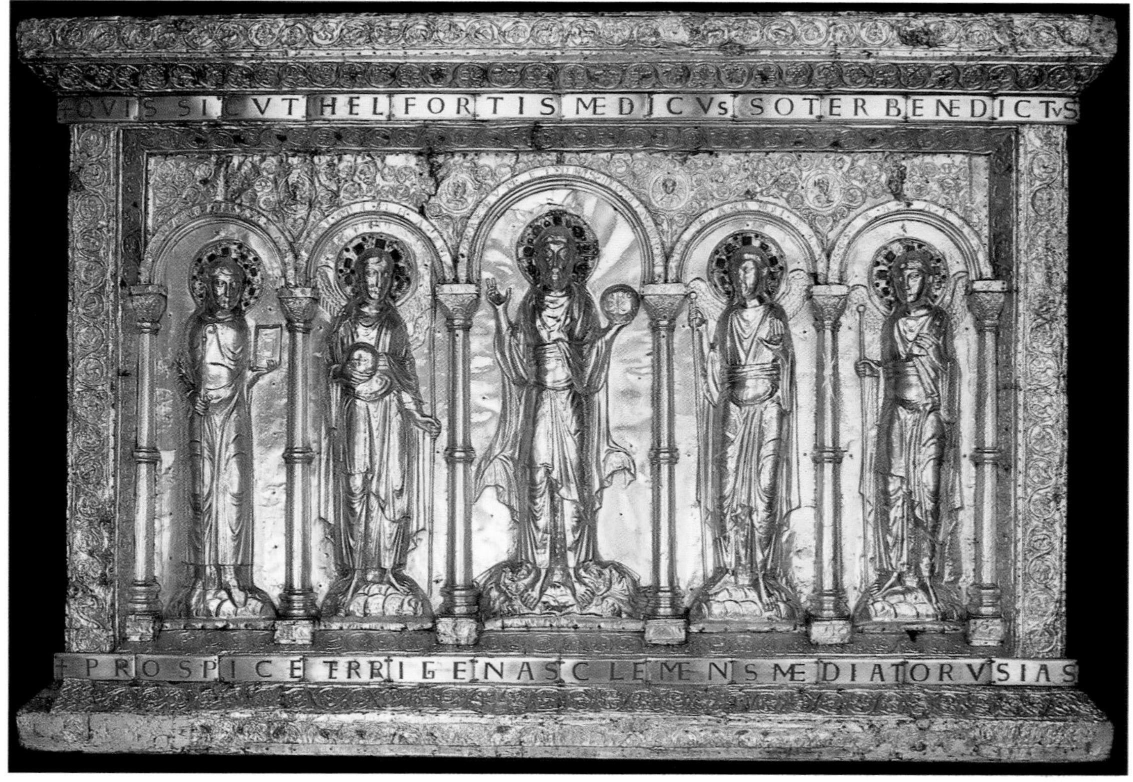

ALMERIA (ANDALUSIA)

Early XIth century

Fragment from the shroud of Saint Lazarus of Autun

Silk, silk and gold thread
H. 0.55 m; W. 0.30 m
C. Côte Collection; donation of M. David-Weill, 1933
Cl. 21865

The dark blue taffeta background is embroidered with polychrome silks and gold threads forming two wheels and two polylobed medallions with gold beads. These embroidered medallions display, in turn, a sphinx, a falconer on horseback carrying a hare, and an eagle with outstretched wings. A wavy decor of embroidered foliated scrolls runs between the motifs. This modest fragment is one of the rare remnants of a Hispano-Moresque fabric reused as a shroud. Saint Lazarus' shroud was found in his grave at Autun around 1147 on the occasion of a translocation of relics. Several pieces were detached from it in the early twentieth century. One such piece is in the Musée historique des tissus in Lyons, another belonged to a private collection before being given to the museum, and the largest, formerly kept in the treasury of the cathedral of Autun, is now in the local city museum. An inscription embroidered on the belt of one of the Autun falconers bears in Kufic script "al-Mozaffar" ("The Victorious"), a title given to the governor Abd-al-Malik after his victory over the Christian army in 1007. The iconography of fantastic animals and the quality of the embroidery establish it as an outstanding product of the Islamic workshops in Spain.

V. H.

The Romanesque world and the rise of the Gothic

Capital from the nave
of the abbey Sainte-Geneviève in Paris
The Twins
Limestone
Circa 1000-1110
Deposit of the École des Beaux-Arts
Inv. 146-198 and WB116

Furthered by a period of peace, the art known as Romanesque blossomed in Europe where societies raised on the classical tradition had the same organization and shared the same faith. The vitality of this art is expressed in architecture, and sustained by the proliferation of monastic orders throughout the Western world. Romanesque art drew the taste for adornment and elegance that we find in ivories and illuminated manuscripts from the Anglo-Saxon world, but from the Islamic world it cultivated an attraction to fantastic bestiary and the genius of reutilization mainly of antique remains. Monumental sculpture offers the richest field. Closely associ-

Heads of King Boson and Saint Stephen
Priory of Charlieu (Loire)
Late XIIth century
Fresco
Cl. 22601 d

ated with its setting, it underscores the main articulations of edifices: capitals, portals, tympani. All of Europe was swept up in this construction dynamic. Yet Paris appears to be an original center, supported by its great monastic institutions, Saint-Germain-des-Prés, Sainte-Geneviève, and Saint-Denis, which were erected near the city gates. Founded by Clovis and Clothilde to house the remains of the patron saint of Paris, the abbey Sainte-Geneviève underwent major development in the early twelfth century. The four capitals of the massive round pillars of the nave, in the museum since the church was torn down in 1807, offer a subtle blend of classicizing inspiration and plastic innovation characteristic of the large Parisian royal buildings. This same classical trend can be observed in the mural paintings that at the time covered the walls of all the sacred edifices. Thus in the burgundian abbey of Charlieu (Loire) eloquent fragments of this art of color can still be seen.

In the Empire, next to monumental constructions the decorative arts express a skillful degree of refinement often achieved in monastic circles with a long artistic tradition. Binding boards, decorated altarpieces, and reliquaries provide magnificent examples. At the opposite of such "elitist" executions, "Limoges work" offered a different production perfectly adapted to liturgical furnishings. The Limousin province, at the time ruled by the Plantagenet dynasty, became the center of a robust and prestigious production that is today scattered all over the world. The Limousin goldsmiths, experimenting with copper champlevé enamel plaques, enamels, and gilding, created utterly beautiful works that reflected the belief of the faithful.

V. H.

PARIS

Second quarter of the XIth century

Christ in Majesty

Capital

Stone (Lutetian limestone)

H. 0.695 m; W. 0.76 m;

D. 0.44 m

From the nave of the abbey of Saint-Germain-des-Prés; lapidary deposit of the City of Paris in 1820; entered the museum in 1844

Cl. 18612

Unlike the Carolingian and Ottonian periods that radically simplified their stone capitals, the eleventh century rediscovered carved decoration, as evidenced by the capitals of Saint-Germain-des-Prés. In addition to floral decorations and scenes from the Old Testament, they feature a cycle devoted to the affirmation of the miracle of Transubstantiation that culminates in a capital representing on its main side the Victorious Christ holding a host in His right hand. Two different sculptors worked together to achieve this program. The one who executed the front with soaring figures carved in relief was influenced by Ottonian goldsmithery, whereas the one responsible for the sides designed much stockier figures rendered in flattened planes.

X. D.

E A S T E R N   F R A N C E   (R H E I M S ?)

Last quarter of the XIth century

Chess-game queen or reliquary (?)

Ivory
H. 0.087 m; Diam. 0.052 m
Possibly from the treasury of the Rheims cathedral;
Du Sommerard collection
Cl. 396

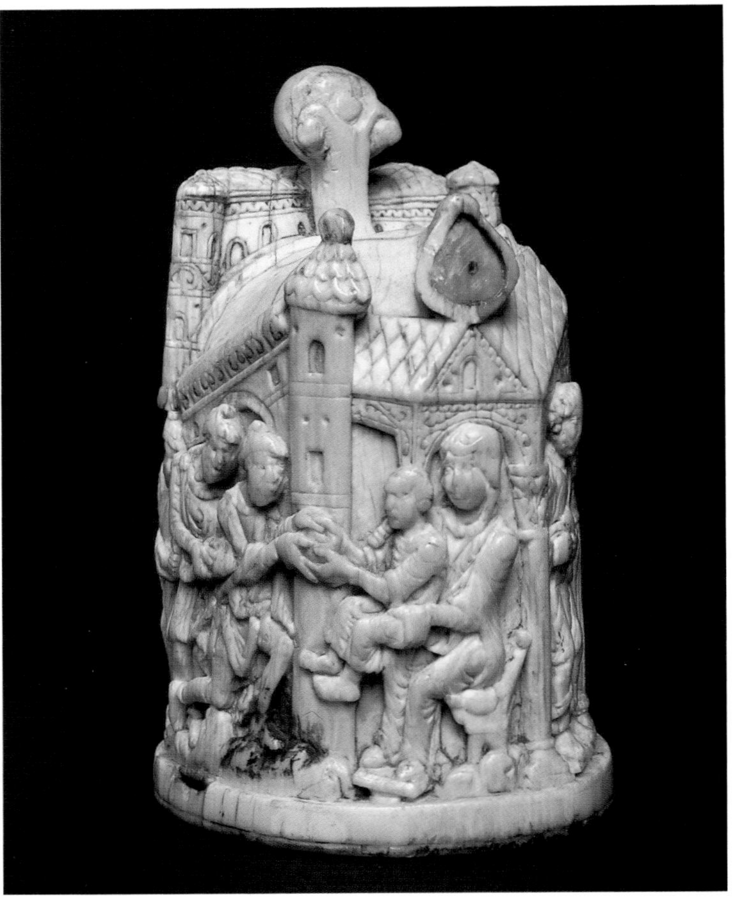

On occasion we must confess our failure to determine the function of an artifact. Such is the case of this complexly shaped small ivory, a masterpiece of carving delicacy. Its bipartite structure, a lower, cylindrical part topped by an upper projecting part, is typical of the chess vizirs (queens) of the late eleventh century, but is also reminiscent of centrally-planned churches. However, since the ivory is hollow and the decoration entirely religious, it may just as well be a reliquary. The lower part is devoted to scenes from the childhood of Christ and His christening. The upper section represents the legend of the baptism of Clovis. This iconography supports the hypothesis that the ivory originated in Rheims, an unsubstantiated attribution given to this piece at the time it entered the Du Sommerard collection.

X. D.

SICILY

Last third of the XIth century

The Ascension

Oliphant
Ivory
H. 0.645 m; W. 0.105 m; Diam. 0.12 m
From the abbey Saint-Arnoul of Metz; Spitzer collection; acquired 1893
Cl. 13065

Oliphants, in the Middle Ages, had multiple functions. Hollowed elephant tusks, they could be used as musical instruments and drinking horns, but others contained relics, which explains why a number of them, like this one, formerly at Saint-Arnoul of Metz, were conserved in church treasuries. It was produced by two artists working together, one was responsible for the decorative bands that derive from Fatimid art, the second for the scenes in the central part, crafted in bas-relief and devoted to the Ascension. This ivory is characteristic of Sicilian workshops of the last third of the eleventh century, whose art is so strongly marked by Byzantine and, above all, Fatimid influences, that it has been suggested they may have employed Saracen slaves.

X. D.

First quarter of the XIIth century

Gospel Book: Traditio legis et clavum

Silver, partly gilded and nielloed, on oak board, parchment
H. 0.283 m; W. 0.204 m
From the cathedral of Novara; Engel-Gros collection; Rütschi collection; Cassel collection; acquired 1954
Cl. 22653

Intended for the deacon charged to proclaim the Word of God during the celebration of the Eucharist, gospel books gather extracts from the Gospels arranged in keeping with the liturgical calendar. The one that was made for the Cathedral of Novara in the early twelfth century was richly decorated with a binding in gilded and nielloed silver on a wooden core. Devoted to Christ entrusting the keys to Peter and the Law to Paul framed by four apostles, the upper band of the central panel reflects the geographic origin and destination of this work. The medallions represent the great saints of northern Italy: Saint Ambrosius of Milan, Saint Eusebius of Vercelli, Saint Syrus of Pavia, Saint Gaudentius and Saint Agabius of Novara. Stylistically, the work shows a strong Germanic influence.

X. D.

IHESVS CRISTVS
IACOBVS
IACOBVS

Circa 1137-1140

Heads of column-statues from the west façade of Saint-Denis

Moses
Limestone
H. 0.40 m; W. 0.23 m;
D. 0.27 m
From the right splaying of the south portal of the west façade of Saint-Denis; removed in 1771; acquired 1988
Cl. 23312

Prophet
Limestone
H. 0.41 m; W. 0.235 m;
D. 0.25 m
From the left splaying of the south portal of the west façade of Saint-Denis; removed in 1771; Rainaut collection; acquired 1992
Cl. 23415

The Queen of Sheba
Limestone
H. 0.365 m; W. 0.21 m;
D. 0.22 m
From the right splaying of the central portal of the west façade of Saint-Denis; removed in 1771; Ozouf collection; acquired 1986

Mentioned as early as the sixth century, the abbey of Saint-Denis's fate was bound to that of the monarchy since Dagobert I's reign. He generously endowed it before being buried there in 639 A.D.. The resting place of several Merovingian sovereigns and of the Carolingians' immediate ancestors, Charles Martel and Pepin the Short, it received, barring a few exceptions, the bodies of most of the Capetians. Although it had been rebuilt at the end of the eighth century and extended in the early ninth century, when Suger was elected abbot in 1122, the abbey still passed for the original construction that, according to legend, Christ himself was supposed to have consecrated. And so when abbot Suger decided to extend the building, he chose not to tear it down, at least not at first, but rather to extend it to the east and the west. This was his opportunity to have the artists that he engaged apply the neo-Platonic artistic theories he had drawn from the writings of the pseudo-Denys Areopagite and the teachings of the school of Saint-Victor. In Suger's view the religious building

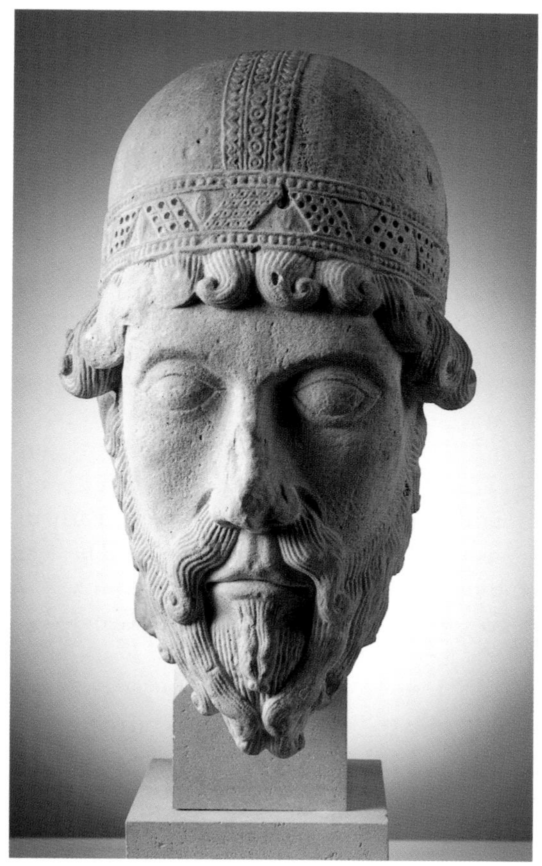

is a total work of art, where architecture, sculpture, stained glass, and goldsmithwork are melded by the essential role of light. This new conception of harmony among the arts gave rise to Gothic art. The three portals of the façade were adorned with a rich carved decoration, and the tympan of the south portal, now lost, was decorated in mosaic. This ornamental program was no longer confined to the tympan, as was the case for the monumental portals of the earlier period, but extended into the frame of the door by the innovative use of a columnar statue.

Subsequently removed in 1771 during an "embellishment" campaign that widened the portals to make room for the processional dais, the columnar statues were decapitated at an unknown date. Six heads from these columns have been located today. Two of them are in the Walters Art Gallery in Baltimore, one in the Fogg Museum of Art at Harvard University in Cambridge, Massachusetts. The remaining three joined the museum collections between 1986 and 1992.

These three heads show that the portals of the west façade of Saint-Denis represent a fundamental stage in the history of medieval sculpture. The hieratic faces and deeply carved features, executed in a technique similar to metalwork, confer on them a remarkable power of expression that was further enhanced for the queen of Sheba, when the eye sockets, which may at one time have contained a vitreous paste, were hollowed out, making the gaze particularly striking.

X. D.

Saint-Denis
Circa 1140-1145

Facing harpies

Capital
Limestone with traces of polychromy
H. 0.261 m; W. 0.412 m; D. 0.30 m
From the cloister of the abbey of Saint-Denis; Maignan collection, acquired 1996
Cl. 23531

Because it has disappeared, we often overlook including the cloister of Saint-Denis among Suger's large Paris yards. However, the fragments that have reached us, in particular the four capitals kept in the museum, prove the care given to this building by sculptors who also worked on the chevet of Saint-Germain-des-Prés. Acquired in 1996, the double capital of the former Maignan collection features two facing harpies on each of its large sides; one bears the face of a beardless man, the other bears a woman's face. Even more than its fantastic iconography, typical in the art of capitals of the early twelfth century, it is the plasticity of the bodies and treatment of the foliage that makes this work exceptional.

X.D.

1140-1144

Two monks witnessing the death of Saint Benedict

Colored glass,
grisaille, lead
H. 0.58 m; W. 0.38 m
From the royal abbey
of Saint-Denis;
acquired 1958
Cl. 22758

The reconstruction of the abbey of Saint-Denis in the twelfth century marks the beginning of a period of prosperity for stained-glass windows. The museum keeps two elements of a window devoted to the life of Saint Benedict, which in the eighteenth century were in the ambulatory of the abbey chancel: one is a piece of the border, the other a figural scene formerly inscribed in a round medallion over a mosaic corner. The inscription on the banderole ("This is the Way whereby the Lord's beloved, the blessed Benedict is risen to heaven") repeats the legendary words uttered at the Saint's death by an angel that we should imagine facing the monks attending the scene. According to fragments found in England, this is the final episode of a window that comprised at least six scenes. The painting, with its rather metallic lines, can be compared to illuminated manuscripts from twelfth-century workshops in northern France.

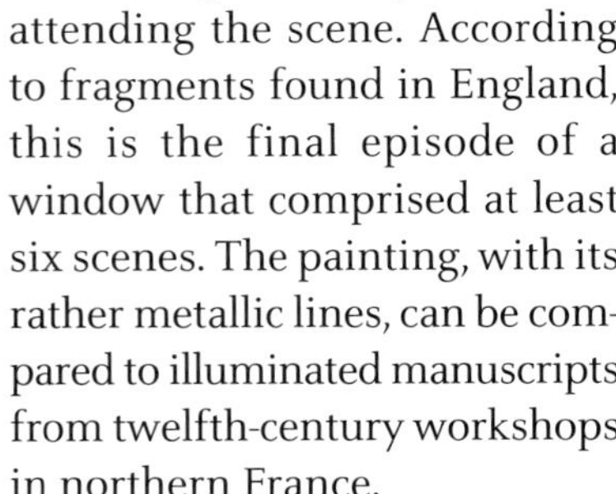

S. L.

P A R I S
Circa 1150

Saint Marcel

Trumeau
Stone (Lutetian limestone)
H. 4.70 m; W. 0.37 m
D. 0.51 m
From the south portal of the façade of Notre-Dame de Paris (Sainte-Anne portal), entered the museum in 1857
Cl. 18640

The Sainte-Anne portal occupies a special place in the history of Notre-Dame. Carved in the middle of the twelfth century for the old cathedral, it was dismounted and reintegrated in the new façade at the beginning of the next century. Its pier was not consecrated to a biblical figure but instead to Saint Marcel, bishop of Paris in the fifth century. It matches the one devoted to another Parisian bishop, Saint Germain, which was placed on the tympanum, and inspired by iconography that glorifies the local Episcopate. The eminent position of this pier can probably be explained by the fact that the cathedral conserved Saint Marcel's relics, unlike those of Saint Germain. Exceptional in quality, this work, with its angular folds rising in close curves over the left arm or loosely falling along the length of the body, demonstrates the virtuosity of the first Gothic sculptors.

X. D.

Circa 1160-1170

Pentecostal Altarpiece

Champlevé, enamelled and gilded copper, brown varnish on wooden core
H. 0.85 m; W. 2.15 m
Mansard collection; acquired for Saint-Denis in 1838; assigned to the museum in 1895
Cl. 13247

The altarpiece represents the episode of the descent of the Holy Ghost on the day of Pentecost, recorded in the Acts of the Apostles (I,2). The figures of the Apostles and of Christ, in flowing drapery, stand out against the gilded copper background. The enamelled haloes enliven the radiant chased gilded forms with touches of color.

Strongly marked by classical influences, this Pentecostal altarpiece is characteristic of the productions of the Meuse valley goldsmiths. It might have originated in one of the most prestigious artistic centers of the Romanesque period, the Benedictine abbey of Stavelot, of which abbot Wibald was a prominent figure in his day. The altarpiece itself belongs to the intellectual and artistic blossoming of the Meuse region. Its quality and erudite iconology represent an art steeped in a theology that closely associated Old and New Testament. Thus it can be read as a symbolic representation of the Church: the Apostles, pillars of the Church, are summoned together by the descent of the Holy Ghost, thereby achieving the constitution of the Church, the house of Wisdom.

E. A.

Champagne Region

Last quarter of the XIIth century

Scenes from the life of Saint Nicholas

Colored glass, grisaille, lead
H. 0.91 m; W. 0.56 m
From Troyes (Aube), probably from the collegiate church of Saint-Étienne; Bacri collection; acquired 1969
Cl. 22849

It was in his main city, Troyes, that Henry the Liberal chose to build a collegiate church near his palace that would become the resting place of the counts of Champagne. He richly endowed the edifice, as evidenced by the dispersed group of stained-glass windows attributed to it. From the life of Saint Nicholas, one of the most popular saints in the twelfth century and portrayed in many medieval windows, the museum keeps two miracle scenes (the Jew lending money in front of the statue of the saint; the saint saving the three daughters of a bankrupt man from prostitution). In a city known for its major fairs, such as Troyes, charity and usury, a new theme, provided the canons with appropriate topics for their sermons.

Located on the borders of the Empire, Champagne artists were receptive to Mosan influences; their minute renderings remind us of illuminated works from late twelfth-century Troyes' artists. These panels stand out as "miniaturists' stained-glass".

S. L.

AUVERGNE
Second half of the XIIth century

Christ on the Cross

Wood is less resistent to the throws of time, but very few sculptures using this support have come down to us. Nonetheless this large Crucifixion, probably made for a glory beam placed over the altar, reveals the extreme refinement achieved by sculptors working in this material. The slight tilt of the head and the partly closed lids give the eyes an expression of sadness that humanize the figure. At the same time, the treatment of the hair and *perizonium* (loincloth), carved with perfect mastery in motifs similar to goldsmithwork, add to its grandeur. Although this work had been once attributed to Burgundy, the few extant documents related to its history confirm it most likely comes from a monument in the north of Auvergne.

X. D.

Polychrome wood
(pear tree?)
H. 1.81 m; W. 1.89 m;
D. 0.28 m
Donation of M. Mallay, 1852
Cl. 2149

VALLEY OF BOÏ (CATALONIA)

Circa 1120-1140

Holy Woman

Pear wood with traces of polychromy, stuffing of the slits with linen fibre
H. 1.33 m; W. 0.31 m; D. 0.38 m
Pitcairn Collection; donated by the ARMMA with the participation of AREVA 2001
Cl. 23673

At the end of the eleventh century, theological disputes over the question of the reality of Christ's death on the Cross arose. To counter the effects of these controversies on the population, the Church emphasized the importance of the liturgy of the Passion and developed a splendid display meant to underscore its significance. Along with liturgical plays, which grew in number and complexity, monumental representations of the Descent from the Cross appeared. The Holy Woman that recently entered the museum collections seems to suggest that the Holy Women at the Tomb must have been another frequent theme. The pendant of a statue kept in the Fogg Museum at Harvard University, this work is the only vestige in France of the talent of an active artist who also executed several Descents from the Cross for the churches of inland Catalonia.

X. D.

Third quarter of the XIIth century

Christ in Majesty

Bookbinding plate
Champlevé, cloisonné, enamelled and gilded copper
H. 0.236 m; W. 0.136 m
Spitzer collection; acquired 1893
Cl. 13070

The enamelled plate, as well as another one representing the Crucifixion (today in Madrid), most likely once adorned the binding of a precious liturgical manuscript. In a mandorla that frames Him in a crown of light, Christ stands out against the gilded ground. Enthroned on the rainbow, holding the Book in His left hand and blessing with the right, He is the Alpha and the Omega. He is surrounded by the symbols of the four Evangelists: Saint Matthew's angel, Saint John's eagle, Saint Mark's lion, and Saint Luke's bull. Christ in Majesty, Christ judge and victor over death, is one of the Romanesque artists' favorite themes, and often shown to the faithful on liturgical objects or church portals.

The question which workshop produced this piece has not been resolved. Stylistically related to the decoration of the large enamelled shrine of Saint Dominic of Silos for the abbey of Silos (Castille), it might also be attributed to the Limoges enamellers' earliest workshops. Its author practiced the technique of champlevé enamel as well as cloisonné with great virtuosity. The perfectly chiselled heads alone were crafted separately.

With its stunning representation of Christ in Majesty, the plate is unquestionably one of the masterpieces of medieval enamel work. Demonstrating a consummate art, the enameller allied brilliant colors with the vibration of the gold and to the ample, whirling forms of the drapery, making this blessing Christ a figure full of power and life.

E. A.

LIMOGES

Circa 1190

Saint Stephen of Muret and Hugo of Lacerta

Plaque from the high altar of Grandmont
Champlevé, enamelled and gilded copper
H. 0.26 m; W. 0.18 m
Du Sommerard collection
Cl. 956 a

In addition to the Adoration of the Magi, also kept in the museum, this plaque representing Saint Stephen of Muret and his disciple Hugo of Lacerta is the only other known vestige of the great altarpiece that used to adorn the high altar of the abbey of Grandmont.

Most likely, the altarpiece was crafted soon after the canonization of Stephen of Muret, who founded the eremetic order of Grandmont in 1077. We know that it combined scenes from the life of Christ with those of the saint who had founded the order, like in this posthumous apparition of Stephen to Hugo of Lacerta, in which the inscription is written in vernacular language.

For the refined decor of the high altar, the Grandmont community turned to the Limoges workshops, which were getting under way at the time. Set on a gold ground, the scene displays the characteristic color scheme of Limoges enamelling, which is based on a subtle use of blue.

E. A.

Late XIth-early XIIth century

Processional Cross with Marian program

Partly gilded and nielloed silver on iron core,
H. 0.73 m; W. 0.39 m
Possibly from Eskisehir (Turkey); acquired 1987
Cl. 23295

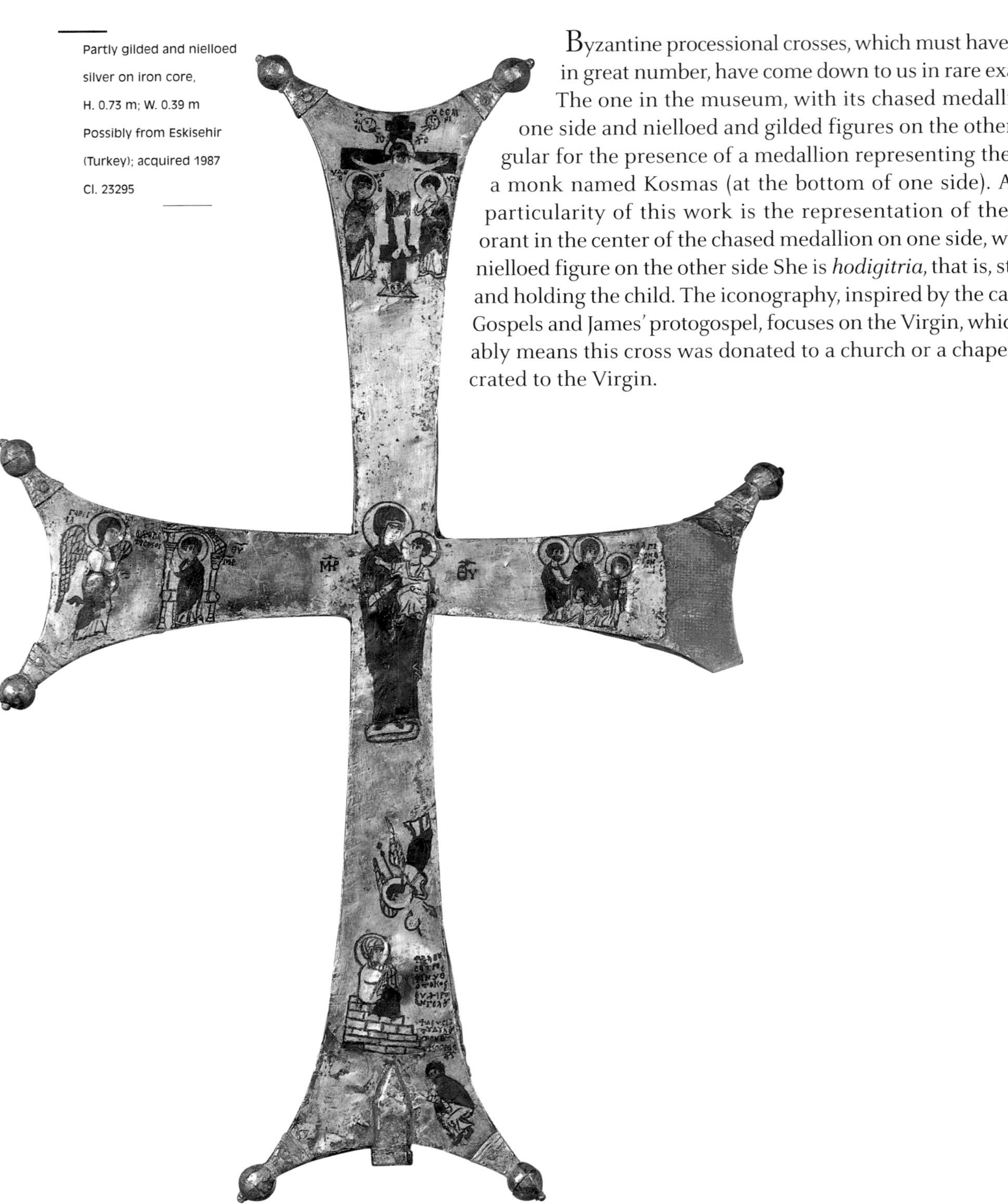

Byzantine processional crosses, which must have existed in great number, have come down to us in rare examples. The one in the museum, with its chased medallions on one side and nielloed and gilded figures on the other, is singular for the presence of a medallion representing the donor, a monk named Kosmas (at the bottom of one side). Another particularity of this work is the representation of the Virgin orant in the center of the chased medallion on one side, while the nielloed figure on the other side She is *hodigitria*, that is, standing and holding the child. The iconography, inspired by the canonical Gospels and James' protogospel, focuses on the Virgin, which probably means this cross was donated to a church or a chapel consecrated to the Virgin.

X. D.

Fragment of the shroud from Saint-Sernin (Toulouse)

Silk samite
H. 0.44 m; W. 0.23 m
Saint-Sernin Basilica,
Toulouse; acquired 1892
Cl. 12869

This magnificent fabric was brought to light when the reliquary of Saint Exuperus was opened, first in 1582 and then again in 1846. Several pieces presently in London, Florence, and Paris were removed at the time. The most important one remains preserved in the treasury of the Toulouse basilica. The decoration consists of rows of facing peacocks spreading their tails in front of a tree of life, separated by an inscription in Kufic that

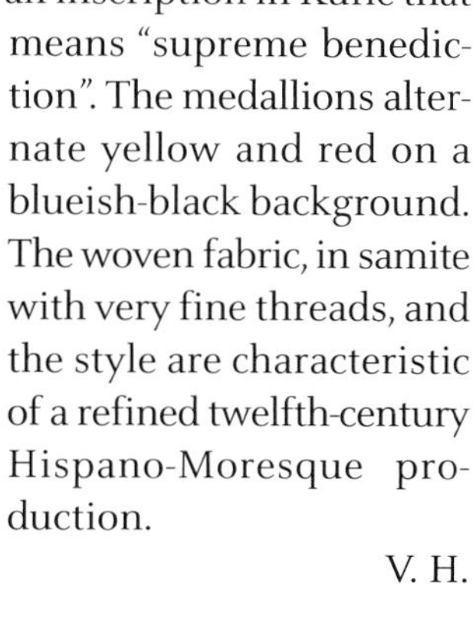

means "supreme benediction". The medallions alternate yellow and red on a blueish-black background. The woven fabric, in samite with very fine threads, and the style are characteristic of a refined twelfth-century Hispano-Moresque production.

V. H.

The XIIIth Century

Cathedral Notre-Dame de Paris:
The Resurrection of the Dead
Lower lintel of the central portal
Limestone
RF 996; Cl. 18643

In architecture, the truest expression of the thirteenth century are the great building programs undertaken by the bishops and abbots supported by a consolidated royal authority. Around 1140 Suger, the abbot of Saint-Denis, revolutionized the architectural conception of his church. A believer in the dignity of royalty and aspiring to elevate the souls of the faithful, he used already proven technical devices, like the pointed arch and the ogival window, to make the wall lighter. This created space for stained-glass windows, reflections of heavenly light. At Saint-Denis, Suger created models such as the chevet with an ambulatory and the façade with three portals that would become references for the new art, soon called *opus francigenum.* This architectural system was applied, without becoming uniform, at the sites connected with the power of the Capetians at the cathedrals of Chartres, Paris, Rheims, and Amiens. After the Gothic of the beginning of the century, a rayonnant Gothic arose that was lighter and more ornamented. At Notre-Dame de Paris, the renovation of the west façade

Trimming the tree hanging over a neighbor's house
Paris, second half of XIIIth century
Miniature on vellum
Cl. 72717 b

involved a program of monumental sculpture that would become exemplary. The central portal was dedicated to the Resurrection of Christ, of which important parts—the Last Judgment—are shown in the museum. Together with them, we can admire the stunning group of heads of the kings of Judah that come from the upper gallery and were "miraculously" rediscovered in 1977. In the mid-thirteenth century, the Sainte-Chapelle in Paris, built by Saint Louis to shelter the relics of the Passion, offered a dazzling display of experiments that sought to give the building the impression of weightlessness and greater luminosity. At the same time, the sculpture program asserted its outstanding plastic quality. Elegance and harmony characterized thirteenth-century Parisian art, particularly when it was associated with a royal commission as at Gercy abbey or Poissy collegiate church.
The decisive development of stained-glass windows occurred during the classical period of Gothic architecture. The painstaking and complex elaboration of the process—cutting out the glass, painting in grisaille, baking, leading—required significant financial means that justified the participation of laymen, especially from the crafts corporations, and which occasionally implied long and drawn out executions. Court art and royal commissions marked the decorative arts. Goldsmithwork and ivory were the favorite materials. First limited to liturgical items—reliquaries, caskets, and devotional statues—they were also used for the nobles' secular art, in caskets and mirrors. Illumination held a privileged position, producing better preserved masterpieces than monumental painting or works on panel. Gothic painters liberated themselves from the Romanesque artists' plastic formalism; they promoted human values and expressed feelings. This evolution can be seen in a greater plasticity of the graphic line and the rise of artists attached to the royal court whose names we now know.

V. H.

N O R T H E R N   F R A N C E   (?)

Circa 1200

Reliquary-casket

Gilded silver, filigree, rock crystal, gems, pearls
H. 0.11 m; W. 0.14 m; D. 0.09 m
Treasury of the cathedral of Moutiers-en-Tarentaise (Savoie); acquired 1887
Cl. 11661

This reliquary illustrates the commercial and artistic exchanges that took place between the East and the West during the Middle Ages. It is the work of a Christian goldsmith who reworked a secular quartz casket created in Egypt in the tenth century. Carving rock crystal was a specialty of Fatimid artists, who executed luxury articles in this rare material.
The plaques, adorned with facing ibexes, a deer, and a dog, were cut out and mounted on a wooden core enhanced with gems and filigree. This example demonstates how an originally Islamic and secular item could be altered for Christian use, a common practice in the Middle Ages. The quartz plaques enabled the faithful to see the precious relics kept in the casket. The style of filigree dates this mounting around 1200.

E. A.

Circa 1200-1210

Reliquary of saint Thomas Becket

Champlevé, enamelled and gilded copper
H. 0.15 m; W. 0.16 m; D. 0.05 m
Cathedral of Palencia (Spain); Rosenberg collection; Chappée collection; acquired 1987
Cl. 23296

At the time of the Lateran Council in 1215, pope Innocent III authorized the use of champlevé enamel for holy vases. "Limoges work" then flourished, providing liturgical articles to the churches of the western world, from Italy to Sweden. Since Limoges production used gilded copper, it offered the attraction of a colored, precious material for a relatively modest cost.

Thus the Limoges goldsmiths were great suppliers of reliquaries, which were usually shaped like a house with a pitched roof. On the main side, the iconography is often the life of the saint whose relics are preserved in the reliquary.

A number of Limoges reliquaries house the relics of Saint Thomas Becket, chancellor of England and archbishop of Cantorbery, assassinated on December 29, 1170 while he was celebrating mass, and canonized in 1173. On this reliquary, whose state of conservation is exceptional, the scene of the murder of Thomas Becket in front of the altar is shown on the side and, on the roof, that of the burial of his body.

E. A.

LIMOGES

Circa 1210-1220

Christ on the Cross

Champlevé, enamelled and gilded copper
H. 0.39 m; W. 0.32 m; D. 0.04 m
Acquired 2001
Cl. 23671

The museum owns one of the finest collections of Limoges enamels in the world, and holds a complete array of the liturgical objects created in Limoges workshops between the late twelfth and late thirteenth centuries that include reliquaries, precious bindings, crosses, croziers, candlesticks, incense-boats, and pyxes.

This magnificent Christ, most likely affixed originally to a large altar cross, is one of the major pieces. He is represented as a glorious Christ, alive, his face serene, wearing the royal crown. The statuette, combining late Romanesque with early Gothic styles, associates monumentality and an extraordinarily plastic manner with elegant lines and a fluid rendering. It is typical of "Limoges work" at the peak of its quality, in which masterful craftsmanship vies with artistic creativity.

E. A.

Lucca (Tuscany)
XIIIth century-early XIVth century

Arnaud de Via's pontifical stocking

Silk, gold thread
H. 0.63 m; W. 0.28 m
Abbey of Villeneuve-lès-Avignon; donation of the Prefect of the Gard, 1867
Cl. 8064

Found in the binding of a manuscript at the abbey of Villeneuve-lès-Avignon, this stocking made from a thirteenth-century silk fabric is a rare piece of liturgical garb which has been connected with Arnaud de Via, who died in 1335. Nephew of pope John XXII and protector of the abbey, he was a well-known figure at the Avignon pontifical court.

The decoration of this item consists of pairs of back-to-back crowned gazelles, separated by palmettos. A swarm of fantastic birds and palmettos throng the space. The heads, feet, several flowers, and cartouches are enhanced in gold. Countless examples of these gold-brocaded lampas are described in inventories. An exceptional piece with the same pattern but brocaded in yellow silk instead of gold is still kept in the treasury of the Sens cathedral. Iconographically and technically, this silk underscores the influence of Islamic workshops on the Italian production of figured silks.

V. H.

TUSCANY

Circa 1220-1230

The Virgin and Saint John at the Calvary

Polychrome cottonwood
H. 1.71 m
From the cathedral of Prato (Tuscany); Du Sommerard collection
Cl. 2368-2369

Like the Auvergne or Catalonia, Central Italy is well known for its outstanding production of painted, gilded wooden statues (Madonna and Child) and monumental groups (Crucifixions). By the early thirteenth century, the mournful and highly suggestive episode of the Deposition seems to have been a favorite of the Italian churches marked by the Franciscan Humanist devotion. The carvings were generally placed above the choir screens.

Associated with the deposed Christ of the cathedral of Prato (Prato museum), the museum's Virgin and Saint John have been compared to the style of the Descent from the Cross in the cathedral in Tivoli. The linear purity and the slenderness of the bodies, still Byzantine, are combined, in the innovative manner of the sculptor Benedetto Antelami from Parma (active between 1177 and 1233), with a certain monumentality in the figures—a gravity in the bodies and the faces that establishes the originality of early thirteenth-century Italian Gothic sculpture.

S. L.

Circa 1230

The Tree of Jesse

Transparent and colored glass, grisaille paint, lead
H. 0.90 m; W. 0.58 m
From the church of Varennes (Essonne), originally in the abbey of Gercy or Jarcy (Essonne) [?]; deposit of the Monuments historiques, 1950
Cl. 23674-23675

During the nineteenth century, in the choir of the small church of Varennes-Jarcy (Essonne), a group of thirteen panels of 13th-century stained-glass were discovered. Everything leads us to the belief that it came from the neighboring abbey of Gercy, established by Jeanne of Toulouse around 1260. One of the stained-glass windows illustrates the theme of the Tree of Jesse inspired by an iconographic formula invented at Saint-Denis in the mid-twelfth century. This theme, which glorifies the royal ancestry of the Virgin and therefore of Christ, was appropriate for a princely Order consecrated to Our Lady. Stained-glass windows of the Tree of Jesse were particularly popular during the reign of the Capetians. Extremely simple, this window, preserved in its upper section, features two prophets, and the Virgin and Christ surrounded by the seven doves of the Spirit. The elongated figures and lively gestures seem to anticipate the linear, functional style of the Sainte-Chapelle in Paris.

S. L.

Heads of the Kings of Judah

Limestone
H. 0.41 to 0.71 m; W. 0.18 to 0.44 m; D. 0.34 to 0.39 m
From Notre-Dame de Paris, west façade, gallery of Kings
Cl. 22988, Cl. 22991, Cl. 23000, Cl. 23002

In its determination to erase every trace of feudalism, the French Revolution systematically and dramatically damaged the monumental decoration of the cathedral Notre-Dame de Paris. In 1793, the twenty-eight statues of the Kings of Judah on the main façade were torn down and sold to a contractor as building stone. Believed lost, they were restituted *in situ* by Viollet-le-Duc's équipe in the mid-nineteenth century. But in 1977, during the construction work rue de la Chaussée-d'Antin, twenty-one heads of Kings—and over a hundred fragments of statues—were fortuitously discovered. The heads had been bought in 1796 and then piously buried. One of the most important archeological finds of these past decades, it largely contributed to our knowledge of Parisian sculpture in the first half of the thirteenth century.

The gallery of Kings overlooking the level of the three west façade portals was carved around 1225-1230. It is the oldest example of a horizontal representation of the kings of Judah, ancestors of Christ by the Virgin, whose statue crowns the gallery. This monumental biblical genealogy—well suited to glorify the image of Capetian royalty—was repeated in the thirteenth century on the façades of the cathedrals at Chartres, Amiens, and Rheims.

The statues, 3.50 meters high, were placed under the trilobate arcades with their architectural decor. The restoration of the cathedral in 1998-1999 confirmed the budding naturalism of their leafy capitals as well as the presence of a bright polychromy that used to cover these sculptures (a contrast of minium reds or red-ochres with blues and greens). Although mutilated by their fall, the heads themselves, colossal in size (0.60 to 0.70 meters high), have kept traces of their color (pink on the cheeks, red for the lips, ochre-yellow heightened with red or blue-gray for the hair and the beard, black for the eyebrows, and black or green for the pupils). Several details seem to have been executed with great care: the crowns, the wavy locks of the hair and beards, and the slightly open mouths. As is the case on the Last Judgment tympanum they overlook, several artists took part in the execution of these heads. One of them (a head known as David, in the lower left foreground) belongs to the simple manner practiced at the beginning of the century in and around Sens, a style also present on the central portal. A less severe vein at Notre-Dame exists as well, especially in the luxurious hair on the head in the upper left foreground, which anticipates the sculptures of the lateral portals at the Paris cathedral and Sainte-Chapelle, and the new mid-century stylistic sensibility.

S. L.

Paris

Circa 1260

Adam

Limestone
H. 2 m; W. 0.73 m; D. 0.41 m
From the cathedral Notre-Dame de Paris, reverse of the south façade of the transept; Saint-Denis storage; assigned to the museum in 1887
Cl. 11657

During the French Revolution, Alexandre Lenoir exhibited a very large statue of Adam in his Musée des monuments français that came from Notre-Dame de Paris. Documents accurately locate the work as having been in a niche with a dais, with Eve as pendant, in the upper part of the back of the south arm of the cathedral transept (drawing by the architect Robert de Cotte in the early eighteenth century). The cathedrals in Rheims and in Bamberg possess similar groups from the same period.

Completed in the nineteenth century, when part of the nose, right arm, left leg and feet as well as the base of the branch were added, the statue has lost the apple it was holding in its left hand. This splendid nude, no doubt derived from an antique, originally polychrome (the vine leaf still has its green coloring), illustrates the naturalistic manner that appeared in the statues of the south portal of the cathedral and in the apostles of the Sainte-Chapelle before it reached the façade of Rheims cathedral.

S. L.

Four figures

Colored glass, grisaille, lead
H. 0.65 m; W. 0.50 m
From the Sainte-Chapelle in Paris, Numbers' window; assigned to the museum in 1855
Cl. 14474

The Sainte-Chapelle, conceived as a huge reliquary, uniquely consists of more glass than mural surface. An immense Bible unfolds on the fifteen windows of the upper chapel. Moralizing rather than theological, the narrative cycle, thronged with crowned figures, is characterized by political shrewdness. The building itself has greatly suffered over time. During the nineteenth century, the damaged, late or non-identified stained-glass windows were removed. That is the case with this panel, which, owing to its shape, appears to come from the window known as the Numbers (counting the tribes of Israel). Its four figures are probably witnesses of one of the window's numerous crowning scenes.

It is characterized by subtle colors and serene faces. The highly expert technique of applying grisaille washes, then delicately brushing them away to create "highlights" at the hem of the garments, comparable to miniaturist techniques, might well be the work of the principle workshop of the Sainte-Chapelle glaziers.

S. L.

Melancholic apostle

Limestone with traces of polychromy
H. 1.65 m; W. 0.52 m; D. 0.43 m
From the Sainte-Chapelle in Paris; deposited in 1797 at the Musée des monuments français, then in 1816 at the Mont-Valérien; assigned to the museum in 1850
Cl. 18665

Built to preserve the relics of Christ's Passion, the Sainte-Chapelle was adorned with a major decorative program. Placed on columns, twelve statues of apostles articulate the interior space, in keeping with the apostolic assembly's innovatory principle widely adopted in the Middle Ages.

In the nineteenth century, the edifice, which was badly damaged in the 1790s during the Revolution, was restored, and the statues considered too mutilated were assigned to the Cluny museum. Since then, the Apostle described as "melancholic" has recovered his head, but still misses his left hand, bare feet, attribute, and his disk marked with a sacred cross. Evidence of the disk having been cut away appear on the bust. The opulence of his garb, formerly polychrome and gilded, the enveloping drapery with its deep folds, the elegance of his curly hair, and his features, which reflect a gentle gravity, testify to a moment of balance and grace, that is, of classicism, that typifies Parisian art in the age of Saint Louis.

S. L.

P A R I S

Circa 1261-1262

Reliquary of Saints Lucian, Maxian and Julian

Gilded silver
H. 0.19 m; W. 0.13 m;
D. 0.02 m
Treasury of the Sainte-Chapelle in Paris; donation of widow Timbal, 1881
Cl. 10746

The reliquary of Saints Lucian, Maxian and Julian is the only one among those made in the age of Saint Louis for the Sainte-Chapelle that eluded destruction during the Revolution. The fragments of the relics of the three saints who brought the Gospel to the region of Beauvais were probably given to the king at the time of their translation in 1261. Created slightly over ten years following the consecration of the Sainte-Chapelle, this reliquary in the shape of a chapel belongs to the artistic style typical of Saint Louis' patronage. The principal side has three apertures that allowed worshipers to see the relics inside. On the back, the architectural decor recalls that of the gallery and baldachin built for the large Sainte-Chapelle shrine. The beautifully modelled figures of saints carrying their heads are exemplary for their vigor and accuracy, attesting to the artistic perfection Parisian goldsmiths achieved in the 1260's.

E. A.

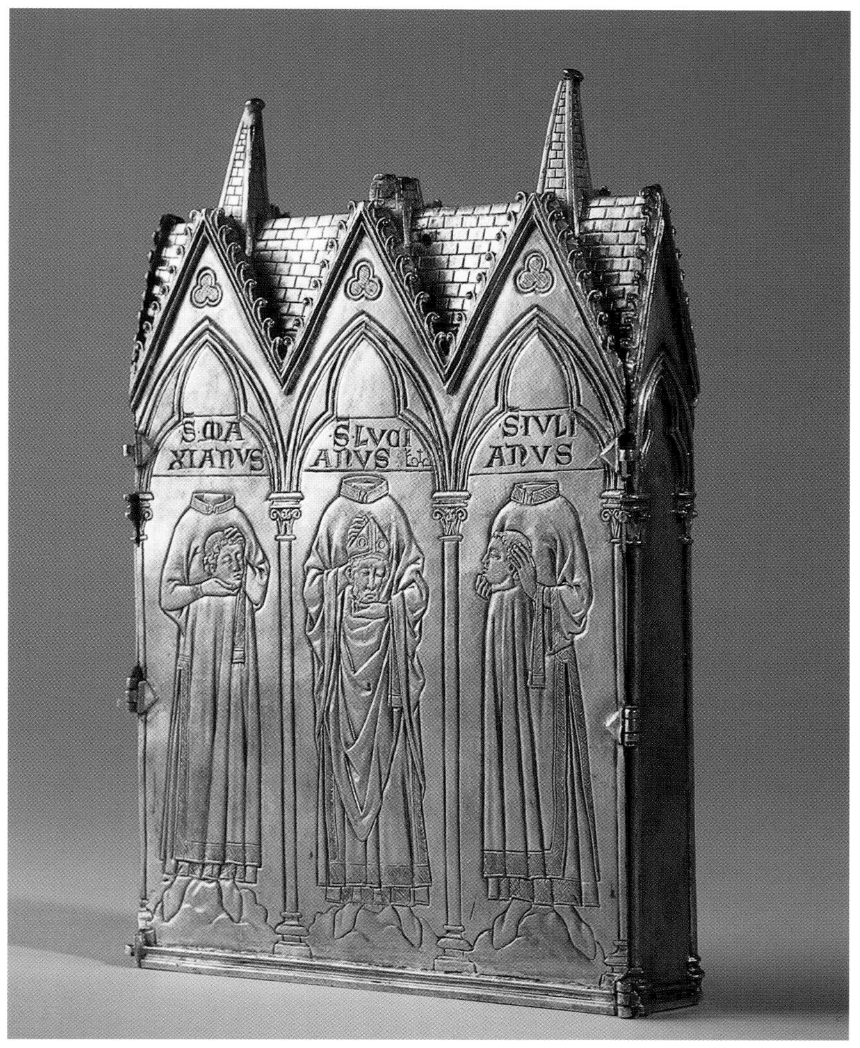

Paris

Circa 1250-1260

Madonna and Child

Elephant ivory
H. 0.52 m; W. 0.165 m;
D. 0.145 m
Barroux collection;
acquired 1851
Cl. 1954

The circumstances leading to the development of ivory work in Paris in the mid-thirteenth century are still obscure. Questions about the supply routes, among other considerations, remain unanswered. In these early days, Gothic ivory workers produced sculptures in the round striking in their similarity to contemporary monumental statuary: several Virgins, including the one in the museum and the Madonna of the Sainte-Chapelle, now in the Louvre, feature the same folds, the same rendering of the eyes and smile as do the Madonnas placed at this time on the pier of cathedrals in northern France, such as the Madonna on the portal of the north transept at Notre-Dame de Paris or the so called Vierge dorée, gilded Virgin, of Amiens.

X. D.

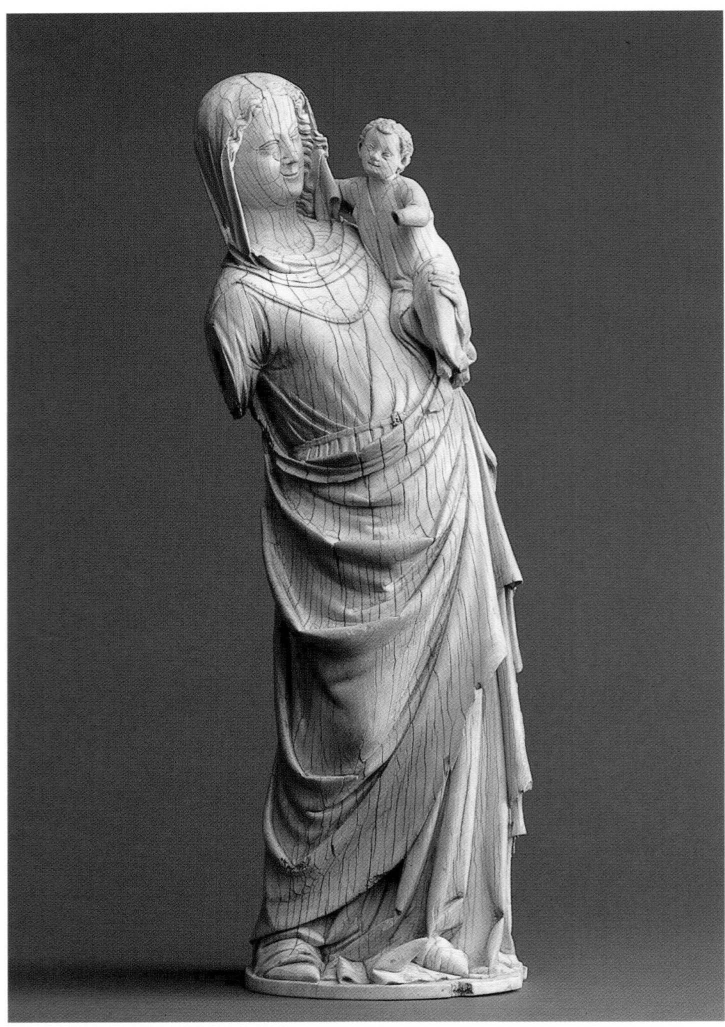

NORMANDY

Circa 1300

Saint Paul

Transparent and colored glass, grisaille, lead
H. 0.7 m; W. 0.6 m
From the royal castle (?) of Rouen (Seine-Maritime); Gorge collection; acquired 1956
Cl. 22728

All that is left *in situ* of the royal castle of Rouen is the donjon. However, four figured panels and several white grisailles (from two different glazing campaigns) come from the site and are now dispersed between Paris, Rouen, and New York. Probably intended for one of the castle chapels, the windows feature the twelve figures of the apostolic college in keeping with the iconographic program at the Sainte-Chapelle in Paris.

Seated on a x-shaped chair with greyhound finials, Paul holds his sword, like the king his sceptre, a posture that recalls various supports, seals, coins, and miniatures from this period that emphasize the sovereign's majesty and dignity. This iconography seems to reflect a royal provenance, all the more so because the quality of the painting, elegance of the figures, subtlety of the poses, and preciousness of the drapery match the finest miniature productions of the 1300's.

S. L.

After 1271

Mask of the funeral effigy of Jeanne de Toulouse

Stone
H. 0.245 m; W. 0.245 m;
D. 0.09 m
From the former abbey of Gercy (Essonne);
Bosquillon collection;
Bourges collection;
Gaubert collection;
acquired 1971
Cl. 22863

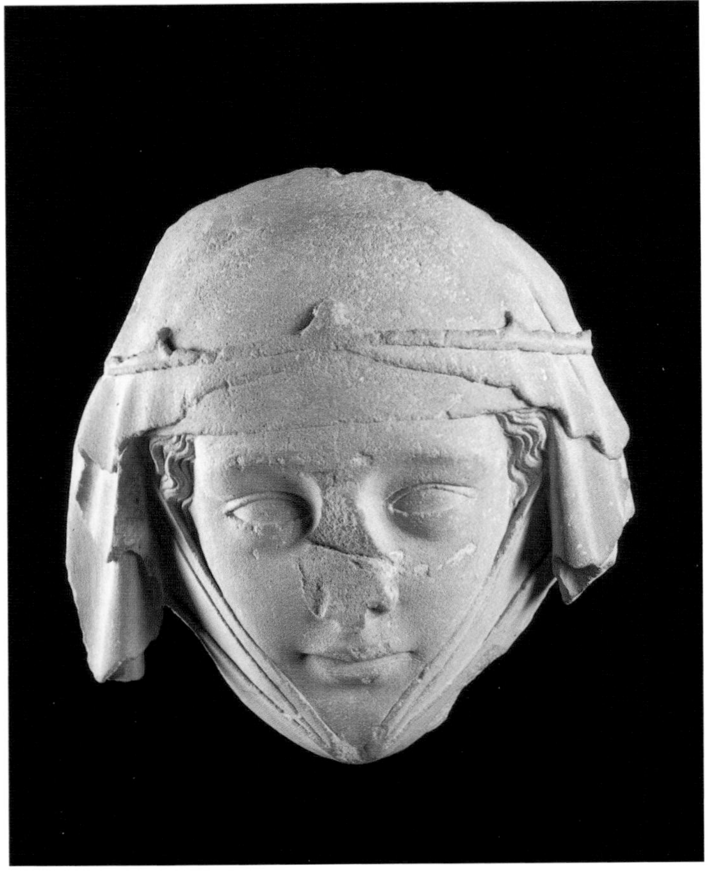

During the first half of the thirteenth century, the apogée for the kingdom of France, the royal family invested in religious foundations while securing for itself worthy burial places. At Saint-Denis, the king launched an important commission for recumbent portraits on tombs to honor his royal ancestors. Not far from his private residence, near Brie-Comte-Robert, Jeanne, the daughter of count Raimond VII of Toulouse and wife of Alphonse of Poitiers, Saint Louis' brother, founded an abbey of canonesses dependent on Saint-Victor in Paris, and decided to be buried there. The abbey disappeared during the Revolution. Commissioned by the king Philip III the Brave, the recumbent figure of the countess (who died in 1271) is known through a seventeenth-century drawing by Gaignères; the mask is all that remains. Of the finest quality, it confirms the superiority of Ile-de-France sculptors. The head, wearing the veil and the chin-piece held by a headband, reveals great sensibility, anticipating the sweetness of turn-of-the-century sculptures.

S. L.

PARIS

Circa 1300

Triptych

Elephant ivory
H. 0.28 m; W. 0.32 m;
D. 0.027 m
From the church
of Saint-Sulpice-la-Pointe
(Tarn); donation of the
church, 1893
Cl. 13101

In the second half of the thirteenth century, polyptychs with religious subjects became the major production of Parisian ivory workers. The one coming from the church of Saint-Sulpice in the Tarn features a classical iconography: a Nativity cycle in the lower register, a Passion cycle in the upper register. The artist who made this proves himself to be a master, demonstrating outstanding technical expertise in a work belonging to the thirteenth-century tradition but that already contains the seeds of future evolutions, particularly in the role the wavy lines and drapery scrolls play in the figures' postures. He also contrasted the deeply hollowed, monumental but solemn figures of the central panel with the lateral scenes, which are in low relief, yet livelier and more compact.

X. D.

Ile-de-France
Circa 1300

Angel bearing the nails and the crown

Limestone with traces of polychromy
H. 1.03 m; W. 0.27 m; D. 0.27 m
From the priory Saint-Louis in Poissy; Bion collection; acquired 1861
Cl. 18762

The canonisation of the king Louis IX was proclaimed in 1297. At Poissy, his ancestor's birthplace, Philip the Fair raised a priory for Dominican nuns based on the architectural model of the abbey of Royaumont, that he then dedicated to Saint Louis. It was completed before 1304. The church transept housed eight free-standing statues of the saint king's family. The museum's angels, and those of the Louvre, hold the instruments of the Passion and are assumed to come from this church. They must have accompanied the figure of Christ at the Last Judgment. But whether they adorned the inside or the outside, the transept wall, the shrine-altar or the west porch, as recently suggested, is not certain. Wrapped in flowing drapery and featuring youthful faces, though not monumental in scale, these angels are a quintessence of the elegance, refinement, and seduction of the art of Philip the Fair's time.

S. L.

THE XIVth CENTURY

The fourteenth century in Europe was an era of prosperity, international exchange, and intellectual and scientific progress as well as a period marred by a series of upheavals: clashes between civic and religious power, dissidence within the papacy, the Hundred-Years' War, and plague. Royal power and court art were closely bound. After Philip the Fair, who died in 1314 and until Charles V, who would live until 1380, artists complied with the demands of their commissioners, who were true patrons. Monumental sculpture was freed from its support. Admirable figures, such as Christ on the Cross, the Madonna and Child, and devotional statues in effigies of various saints, abounded.

The perception of nature led to a highly realistic floral and animal decoration that also involved the representation of civil personalities, especially in funerary art. This elegant, florid style left its mark on goldsmith work, as precious metals were beautifully blended with the subtle colors of enamels. French production denoted refinement and delicacy. Ivory work, for which Paris was a renowned center, was extended to secular luxury items like mirrors, combs, and caskets.

At the end of the fourteenth century, Burgundy was the greatest center of attraction for sculpture. While the center was indeed Burgundian, due to the role played by the four princes of the Valois family, the diffusion of this art was international. Artists from northern Europe appeared on the creative scene, reviving a declining art. Social transformations and upheavals

Reliquary-bust of a companion of Saint Ursula
Cologne, circa 1340
Polychrome wood (limewood)
Cl. 11306

incited the faithful to assert their belief. The great pilgrimage and devotional sanctuaries expanded. Thus at Cologne, the worship of Saint Ursula and her martyred companions assumed an inventive form: the relics were preserved in polychrome, gilded wooden busts of young virgins. Political disturbances did not prevent travel or the circulation of goods: sumptuous velvets from Italy, famous embroideries from England, and bronze or brass items from the Holy Empire were widely diffused. Suggesting greater private devotion, places of pilgrimage now produced on a near to industrial scale badges the faithful took home with them.

V. H.

"Plique" enamels

Paris, circa 1300

Translucent and opaque enamels on cloisonné gold

Cl. 21387, 23411 (a,b,c,d)

PARIS
Circa 1300

The Assembly

Mirror frame

Ivory

Diam. 0.138 m

Du Sommerard collection

Cl. 404

In the late thirteenth century, secular articles in ivory had grown increasingly popular. Along with caskets, knife handles, stylets and writing tablets, mirror frames, particularly distinctive items for an aristocracy ever more sensitive to refinement and fashion, multiplied. They consisted of two small plaques, one of which bore on its inner side a sheet of polished metal, fitted together by a circular motion. The outer sides were adorned with secular motifs, as in the one shown here. The scene, which has not been precisely identified, represents a king and queen surrounded by courtiers crushing the lion and dragon under their feet, while they are looked over by an angel. The mirror frame is as exceptional in size as it is in its precocity and craftsmanship, indicating it was an item intended for a Court.

X. D.

1326-1327

Saint James the Great

Stone

H. 1.75 m; W. 0.58 m

Church Saint-Jacques-de-l'Hôpital (Paris); Pommateau collection; acquired 1852

Cl. 18756

An apostolic college enhanced the church of the hospital Saint-Jacques-aux-Pèlerins, founded in 1319 by the royal family and the Parisian *bourgeoisie,* to host pilgrims on their way to Compostela.

The accounting records of the establishment tell us who sculpted the twelve apostles, of which only the five in the museum remain. Guillaume de Nourriche carved two between 1319 and 1324, and Robert de Lannoy executed the rest of the college between 1319 and 1327. He carved in particular the Saint James, identified by his scrip stamped with a shell.

The apostle's drapery with flattened folds creates a new silhouette, typical of the early fourteenth century: a rather skimpy body compared to the head with its abundant hair, narrow shoulders, very flat bust bared by the movement of the mantle that, drawn over the breast, ripples and flows down the side, adding curves to the lower part of the body. The wide faces, framed in curls falling in supple waves, have a sweet, dreamy expression.

E. A.

P A R I S

Circa 1370-1380

Presentation in the Temple

Marble

H. 0.63 m; W. 0.45 m

Du Sommerard collection

Cl. 18849

In the time of Charles V, the "wise king", Paris was an extremely active artistic center, where artists converged from all over. This relief, which shows the Presentation of Jesus in the Temple and was most likely part of an altarpiece adorned with scenes of Christ's Childhood, has been attributed to both André Beauneveu and Jean de Liège, two of the leading artists of Parisian production during the last quarter of the fourteenth century.

It illustrates the ruling taste for refined simplicity in the handling of the polished marble. The scene, representing the episode in which the elder Simeon recognizes the Savior as the infant in swaddling clothes presented to him by the Virgin, is treated with great plastic vigor and a rare delicacy in expressing the figures' emotions.

E. A.

PARIS (?)

Circa 1350-1370

Mitres from the Sainte-Chapelle

Mourning or Lent mitre

Silk, India ink

H. 0.35 m; W. 0.31 m

Lenoir collection; deposit of the Archives Nationales, 1892

Cl. 12924

Embroidered mitre

Silk, silver and gold thread, pearls

H. 0.37 m; W. 0.30 m

Lenoir collection; deposit of the Archives Nationales, 1892

Cl. 12923

The mitre is one of the privileges of Church pastors, in particular bishops. These two miraculously preserved headdresses come from the treasury of the Sainte-Chapelle and have appeared in the inventories since 1480.

The embroidered mitre, with its gold-threaded architectural and floral forms, its pearls, and pieces of colored glass, imitates goldsmithwork. Surrounding the representation of the apostles and mitred bishop, probably the donor, the Nativity appears under the Crucifixion; on the back, the Adoration of the Magi appears under the Annunciation. The shape of the mitre, the style of the holy figures, and the scenes depicted with a certain realism—especially the bathing of the Child—date this work to the second half of the fourteenth century.

The mitre painted in India ink, a less precious medium, offers a valuable piece of information regarding ordinary liturgical garb. The scenes of the Deposition and Resurrection are painted with a bold hand on white silk, and intended for the period of Lent. The distinctive draughtmanship in some of the figures recalls a famous Parisian work of the fourteenth-century, the *Narbonne Altarcloth* kept in the Louvre, which depicts king Charles V and his wife. In the painted mitre we recognize a follower of the famous Parisian miniaturist Jean Pucelle.

V. H.

Reliquary-portrait of Saint Geneviève

Punched and gilded silver, translucid basse-taille enamels on silver
H. 0.081 m; W. 0.066 m
Louis XIV (?) collection; Royal School of Saint-Cyr; acquired 1989
Cl. 23314

At once a jewel and a devotional object, this precious little reliquary is typical of the cult of saints in the late Middle Ages. Devotional image on one side, reliquary on the other, it could be worn as a pendant, hung on a thin chain. The most refined techniques of late fourteenth-century Parisian goldsmithwork are applied here: translucid basse-taille enamels on silver for the figures, and punched foliated scrolls for the background and the plaque on the back protecting the relics.

Saint Geneviève, the patron saint of Paris, is shown in the traditional episode of the burning candle; above her, to her left, a small black devil shifts about trying to snuff her candle with bellows, while to her right an angel, carrying a small candle, lights it again. The scene symbolizes the struggle between day and night, between good and evil.

E. A.

TUSCANY

Third quarter of the XIVth century

Angel of the Annunciation

Polychrome wood

H. 1.77 m; W. 0.62 m;

D. 0.45 m

Timbal bequest, 1881

Cl. 12560

In the fourteenth century, churches in Italy, as all over the West, were thronged with statues of saints. Central Italy, and particularly Tuscany, had a predilection for carved wood enhanced by a subtle polychromy.

This monumental angel originally belonged to an Annunciation group, of which the Virgin has been lost. The representation of the apparition of the angel Gabriel to the Virgin announcing to her that she is to be the Savior's mother was extremely popular in Italy in the late Middle Ages, and several of these groups still exist, complete or dismembered. This elegant sculpture of the angel Gabriel has been attributed to the workshop of Nino Pisano, one of the most famous Tuscan sculptors of the third quarter in the fourteenth century.

E. A.

Minucchio da Siena

1330 (filigree knot: third quarter of the XIIIth century)

Golden rose

Gold, colored glass

H. 0.60 m

Treasury of the Basel cathedral; gift of colonel Theubet, 1854

Cl. 2351

The museum's golden rose is the oldest extant example. The tradition of these precious objects goes back to the eleventh century, but there are very few medieval golden roses that have outlived the centuries. We know, from the texts, that the creation and gift of one of these roses coincided with a precise consecration. Every year, the fourth Sunday of Lent, or *Laetere* Sunday, the pope blessed a golden rose that was scented with balsalm and musk; he then wore it throughout the liturgy and pronounced a sermon connected with this flower. After which the pope offered the golden rose to a personality he wished to honor.

Thanks to the wealth of information held in the accounting archives of the Avignon papacy, the museum's golden rose has been identified as the one commissioned in 1330 by the Pope John XXII to a Siennese goldsmith working in Avignon, Minucchio da Siena. Indeed, at that time the pontifical court, owing to the popes' munificence and patronage, was one of the leading artistic capitals of Europe, where very different artists, especially French and Italian, converged.

In 1330, Pope John XXII offered the rose to Rudolph III of Nidau, Count of Neufchâtel (who had his enamelled coat-of-arms and a foot added to it). He was a political ally of the pope in his struggle with the emperor Louis of Bavaria. So this elegant object was not merely a reward for religious deeds.

Nonetheless the rose is laden with the rich symbolism of Christian spirituality: the red rose recalls the blood of Christ and the martyrs. More generally, the rose suggests purity and is, *par excellence*, the flower adorning Paradise. According to the first Christian authors, thornless roses blossomed in Paradise as thorns did not appear until after the Fall and man's eviction from Paradise. Thus the rose created by Minucchio da Siena, with its exquisite petals and delicately cut-out leaves, but bare stalk, is very probably a reminder of this heavenly flower, the mystic rose formed by the reunion of saints in Paradise.

E. A.

Between 1330 and 1340

Embroidery with leopards

Silk, partially gilded silver thread, cabochons, pearls
H. 0.51 m; W. 1.24 m
From the abbey of Altenberg-sur-Lahn (Hesse); Solms-Braunfels collection; Heilbronner collection; acquired 1922
Cl. 20367

The five fragments of this decorative fabric arrived in the museum mounted as liturgical garments. But a careful analysis suggests they may come from a ceremonial horse-cloth most likely commissioned by the king of England, Edward III. An outstanding embroidered heraldic decoration unfolds on a red velvet ground: "*léopards passants, armés et lampassés*". Embroidered with gold threads and polychrome silks, the work places courtly scenes amidst elegant foliated scrolls. Extraordinarily inventive and free, and expertly crafted, these embroideries illustrate the *opus anglanicanum*, the consummate art of English embroiderers, at the time held to be the finest in Europe. Gold thread, pearls, glass cabochons, and subtle combinations of colored silks contribute to the beauty of the article. Stylistic comparisons, in particular in heraldry, point to its proximity with the Black Prince's mourning dress, conserved in Canterbury, or psalm-book miniatures of the 1340's.

V. H.

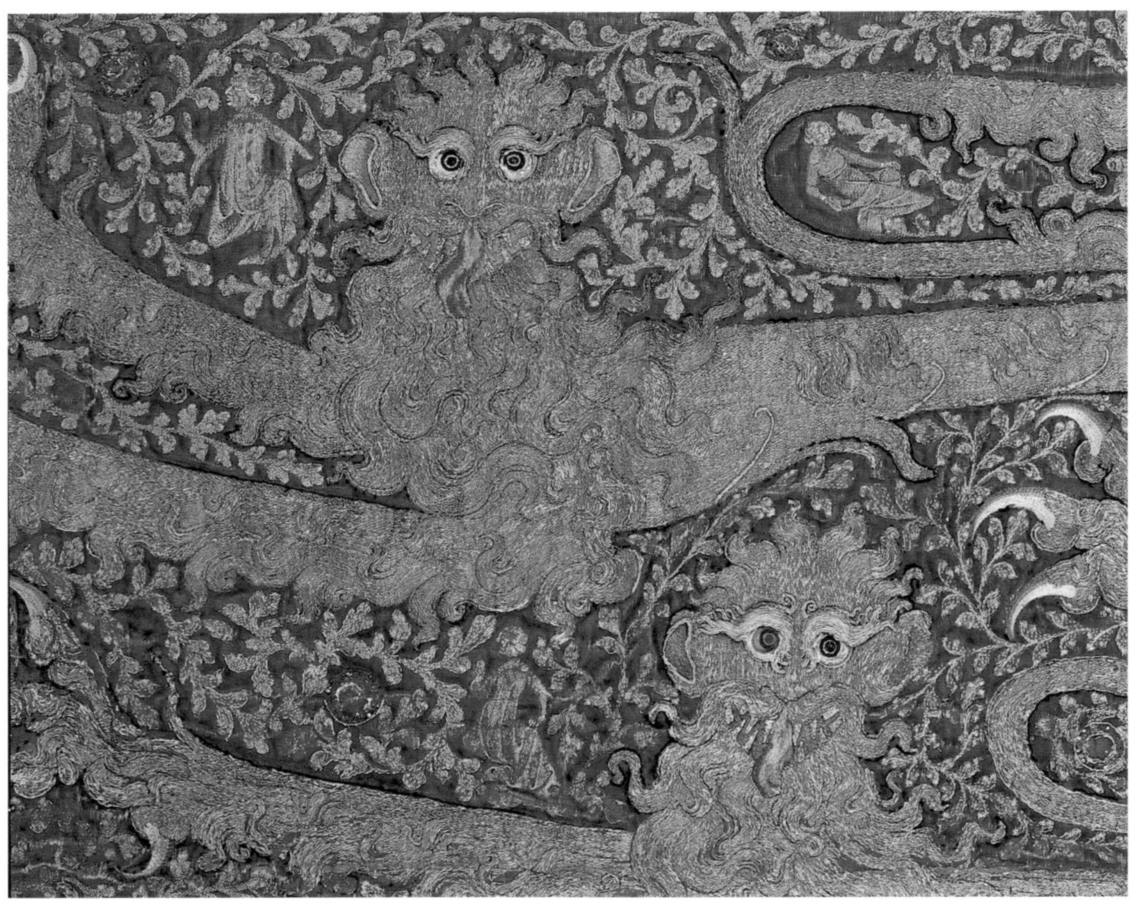

E N G L A N D

Circa 1335

Scenes from the life of the Virgin

Altar front
Painted oak panel
H. 0.75 m; W. 2.85 m
From the church of the Dominican convent of Thetford (Suffolk); acquired 1864
Cl. 7726

The scenes from the life of the Virgin arrived at an early date in the museum collections (though we should mention the loss of the Annunciation). They have been linked to an altar panel of a church in Suffolk featuring the Crucifixion surrounded by figures of saints, mostly belonging to the Dominican order. The same size and displaying the same background decoration, they were in the church of the Dominican priory of Thetford (Suffolk). We recognize the order of Saint Dominic's particular devotion to the Virgin, and the insistence on the highly sensitive theme of the education of the Virgin by Saint Anne.

Very few fourteenth-century painted panels have reached us. This one is particular in that it is an early example of a decoration that incorporated metal foil, the small stamped geometric patterns were applied to tinfoil, polychromed and gilded with gold leaf. The style of the figures reminds us of the mural paintings at the church of Brent Eleigh (Suffolk), dated to 1330.

S. L.

Circa 1330

Carpet window with maple leaves and Crucifixion

Colored glass, grisaille and lead
H. 0.85 m; W. 0.35 m
Supposedly from a church in Colmar (?); donation of Mrs. Montreuil, 1899
Cl. 13747

In the late thirteenth-early fourteenth century, the Rhine valley underwent a major economic and urban evolution. The revival of piety, for example, inspired an intense building campaign. Those were the days of the hall churches with high choirs, vast naves, and countless, huge windows, which resulted in an important movement in window-making.

The Cistercians were followed by the mendicant orders, who addressed the faithful in the cities and to whom they recommended the practice of personal piety. Without adopting the absolute Cistercian austerity, the Franciscans' general Chapter in Narbonne (1260) forbade all figuration, except for the Christ on the Cross surrounded by saints for choir windows. Though these recommendations privileged installing white grisaille windows, by 1280-1300 we observe a return to bright colors, reds and blues, as in the Strasbourg cathedral. The fourteenth century is the era of windows steeped in color that benefit from the quality of "Germanic" window glass. Their naturalist ornamentation is displayed over large surfaces, which explains their being called "carpet-windows"

Framed by a decor of maple leaves, under a tabernacle and architectonic gable, the scene of Christ on the Cross is attended by a non-identified friar donor. The repetition of the same decorative and figurative themes in the Rhine valley—we shall only mention the Mutzig choir axis window —makes its attribution even more arduous.

According to a photograph prior to 1899, this stained-glass window was supposedly in the church of the Colmar Dominicans, but the windows of that edifice are too wide to have contained it and the church already has a window with Christ on the Cross. Other sources suggest that it might come from the Franciscans' church, but neither the donor's white habit nor the size of the maple leaves, much smaller than the ones still there, plead in favor of that assumption. Similar ornamental panels can be seen at Brandenburg Cathedral and in the museum of Nuremberg, but it is the ones in the Munich museum whose provenance is uncertain (Colmar, Franciscans' church?), that follow an identical model. Therefore, we shall maintain that this stained-glass ensemble shares the motifs, with some variations, of the workshops of glaziers on both sides of the Rhine. This is one of the finest examples extant.

S. L.

B o h e m i a (?)
Mid-XIVth century

Clasp-reliquary

Silver, gilded silver, enamels, gems, pearls
H. 0.185 m; W. 0.185 m
Debruge-Duménil collection; Soltykoff collection; acquired 1861
Cl. 3292

This clasp or *cape morse,* impressive in size, was intended to fasten civil or religious formal apparel. On a gilded ground incised with stylized flames an eagle with outstretched wings stands out; he is entirely covered with gems, mainly garnets and sapphires. The plaque, also adorned with gems and pearls, is set inside an enamelled octolobe, rhythmed by small relic-boxes, presently empty.

The technique used for mounting precious stones dates the work to the mid-fourteenth century. The representation of the eagle on a ground of flames, an attribute of saint Wenzel, protector of Bohemia, as well as the eagle's imperial crown, leads us to assume that the clasp might have been executed for a Germanic emperor of the family of Bohemia. He might be Charles IV of Bohemia, emperor from 1346 to 1378 and a passionate relic-lover.

E. A.

FRANCE (?)
XIVth century

Pilgrims' Badges

Our-Lady of Boulogne
Lead and cast tin
H. 0.039 m; W. 0.038 m
Forgeais collection;
acquired 1861-1862
Cl. 4693

Saint Geneviève
Lead and cast tin
H. 0.070 m; W. 0.023 m
Forgeais collection;
acquired 1861-1862
Cl. 5026

Saint George
Lead and cast tin
H. 0.055 m; W. 0.057 m
Gay collection;
acquired 1909
Cl. 18003

Saint John the Baptist
Lead and cast tin
Diam. 0.041 m
Gay collection;
acquired 1909
Cl. 18000

Saint Denis
Lead and cast tin
H. 0.049; W. 0.039 m
Gay collection;
acquired 1909
Cl. 18015

Italy (?) XIVth century
Volto Santo of Lucca
Carved black shist stone
H. 0.086 m; W. 0.047 m
D. 0.023 m
Acquired 1932
Cl. 21590

This selection of badges, all found in the river Seine during the nineteenth century and dating to the fourteenth century, the period in which they were the most common, offers a good illustration of the imagination of those who made these modest devotional articles, which are souvenirs as well as proof of having accomplished the pilgrimage.

Our Lady of Boulogne recalls the miraculous arrival in the harbor, in the early sixth century, of a ship "with neither sailors nor oars" that had on board only the sculpture of the Madonna and Child. The patron saint of Paris, Saint Geneviève is shown here wearing a fleur-de-lis crown. The demon perched on her shoulder unsuccessfully strives with bellows to blow out the candle she holds in her left hand. Saint George is the hero of a very lively scene showing the dragon he slays as well as the princess holding the monster on a leash. Saint John the Baptist's head is placed in the center of a round badge. It is presented like a shield by a priest flanked by two servants. Although comparable to a reliquary, the bust of Saint Denis placed between two angels carrying what appears to be a martyr's palm seems monumental.

This kind of mould was widely used for producing near-industrial quantities of small devotional objects. Thanks to its inscription, the provenance of Lucca seems certain; the Tuscan city was famous for its Crucifix showing Christ wearing a long tunic (*Volto Santo*) and known since the eleventh century. Each arm of the Cross ends with a small attachment ring.

J. F.

FRANCE
Mid XIVth century

Alms-purse, known as the Countess of Bar's

Silk, metal threads
H. 0.36 m; W. 0.32 m
Abbey of Saint-Mihiel (Meuse); purchased at the Delaherche sale in 1888
Cl. 11787

The alms-purse, whose upper part is shaped like a rounded trapezium, is adorned with three allegorical figures embroidered on the velvet ground: a creature, part-youth part-lion, is striking kettledrums, a lion woman with bird's wings is loosely holding a bridle bit and a bearded man with a lion's body is carrying a basket. This secular iconography is usually held to symbolize the vices: the youth would represent vanity, the woman frivolousness, and the elder cupidity. It was widely diffused in the fourteenth and fifteenth centuries. This purse, purchased by the museum with another identical one (Cl. 11788), is believed to come from the Benedictine abbey of Saint-Mihiel. The two pieces were supposedly donated by a certain Countess of Bar. The tradition cannot be verified, but it is not unusual to find secular items in church treasuries. At Troyes, Sens, and Xanten there are objects presenting the same shape and relief embroidery. These refined works are attributed to the mid-fourteenth-century Parisian production.

V. H.

Aquamanile

Cast and engraved bronze

H. 0.22 m; W. 0.19 m

Du Sommerard collection

Cl. 990

Made for religious and secular use, receptacles for containing water to wash one's hands were very common; they frequently show animals, real or chimerical. Here, the representation of the bust of a youth is all the more unusual and interesting in that it has been associated with the bust of a young woman, probably from the same workshop and now kept at Opava (Slovakia).

We should point out the exquisite rendering of details, such as the wavy hair and the foliage frieze trimming the neckline. In the middle of the forehead, the spout for pouring water is framed in festoons, and, on the back, the handle is in the shape of a dragon. As for the escutcheon stamped with a *fleur-de-lis*, we have no way to explain it.

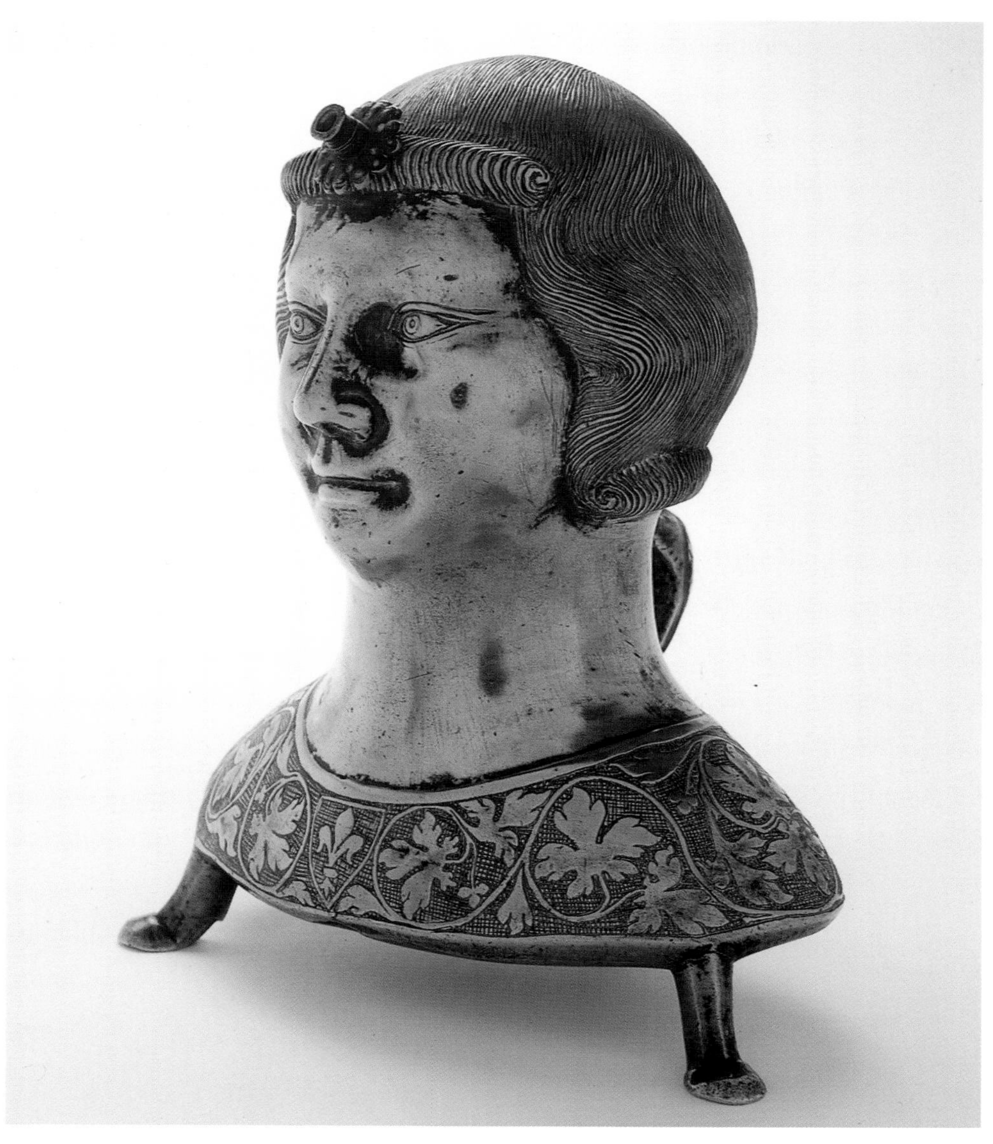

The features, characterized by almond shaped eyes and the hint of a smile, as well as the hairstyle, date this bronze to the early fourteenth century.

J. F.

F L A N D E R S

Late XIVth CENTURY

Casket

Chased, chiselled, painted and gilded leather on a wooden core, brass fittings
H. 0.12 m; W. 0.26 m; D. 0.18 m
Acquired 1910
Cl. 17506

The true symbolism of this casket, in all likelihood an engagement or wedding present, only acquires full significance once the lid is opened. Seated in a enclosed garden, the Madonna and Child reflect the courtly scenes figured on the outside: in this way the Mother of Christ is identified with the beloved. The latter is shown facing her lover, exchanging with him something that may be a flower, her belt, or a ring. The figures, rendered in relief, are set amidst a foliated or landscape background suggested by small grassy hillocks and stylized trees.

Religious iconography and themes of courtly love are associated here, completed by an inscription inviting to meditative devotion. Other caskets of similar style, all created in the same region around 1400 but which illustrate solely religious subjects, do not have this twofold iconography.

J. F.

THE XVth CENTURY

Throughout the fifteenth century, a period in Italy when new conceptions of the Renaissance had already taken shape, a flamboyant style characterized French religious and secular building, exemplified by the cathedrals of Bourges, Sens, Troyes, and by the "Wonder" of the Mont Saint-Michel. The same profusion of wavy lines and ornament was displayed in secular buildings like the mansion of Jacques-Cœur in Bourges, the Cluny mansion in Paris, and the law courts in Rouen.

Marked by the conflicts of the Hundred Years' War, which ended in 1435, society presented a new countenance. Even though the rural world prevailed, people of means began to take over. The development of towns, trade, and "business" brought a new wealth that was to advantage France, Italy, the Holy Roman Empire and Spain. New patrons appeared and new crafts developed that revived artistic practices such as easel painting in Italy and Flanders, wooden altarpieces in the Lowlands and alabaster ones in England, weaving and ivory work in Italy, and widespread book-making. If the delightful illuminated prayer-books that continued to multiply encouraged private devotion, the invention of

Workshop of Balthazar Embriachi:
Altarpiece of Champmol
Before 1393
Bone and marquetry
Cl. 17051

printing diffused new knowledge and ideas. In the course of the century, easel painting flourished, defining the status of the artist. Rogier Van der Weyden, attached to the court of Brussels, like Jean Fouquet, bound to the court of France, are outstanding personalities.

In the Germanic empire, important creative centers, especially in the field of sculpture, were of note. The works of the "fine style", featuring flowing lines and a gentler humanism, tended toward expressionism, where the artists had a preference for bright colors and more angular renderings.

Tapestry remained the major art of the period. Produced by dint of princely patronage, only a few rare luxurious ensembles executed in the fourteenth century, such as the *Apocalypse*, commissioned by Louis of Anjou and presently kept at Angers, still exist. In the fifteenth century, the centers of Bruges, Antwerp, and Brussels, connected with the house of Burgundy, were famous for their abundant production. The weavers invented the "millefleurs" decor, forming the background for religious or courtly scenes. *The Lady with the Unicorn* is its most celebrated example.

V. H.

Hans Greif: Statue-reliquary of Saint Anne the Trinitarian
Ingolstadt, 1472
Partly gilded and painted silver
Cl. 3308

Salzburg (?)

Circa 1395-1400

Pietà (Madonna of Pity)

Polychrome limestone
H. 0.39 m; W. 0.28 m;
D. 0.20 m
Carl collection;
acquired 1999
Cl. 23656

Pietà groups (*Vesperbilder* in German), touching pendants to the Madonna and Child, multiplied in the last centuries of the Middle Ages, becoming one of the favorite images of a devotion that emphasized Christ's sufferings. This theme had a special diffusion and popularity in Germanic countries: the group of the Mother of God and her dead son, disconnected from notions of space or time, was the privileged mainspring for meditation on Christ's death, inspired by mystical poetry.

These images abounded around 1400 in central European international Gothic sculpture, where the "fine style" flourished. The museum's Madonna of Pity is a perfect example of this style, derived from the Parlers' workshops in Prague. The sculptor figures the Virgin with great sweetness, as a very young maiden. Only the tears running down her cheek underscore her immensely sad glance. Poignant grief is entirely interiorized, and it is this very restraint that produces the group's emotional impact. In mystical terms, the Virgin represents the soul of the Christian receiving in his bosom the wounded body of Christ and meditating on his salvation.

E. A.

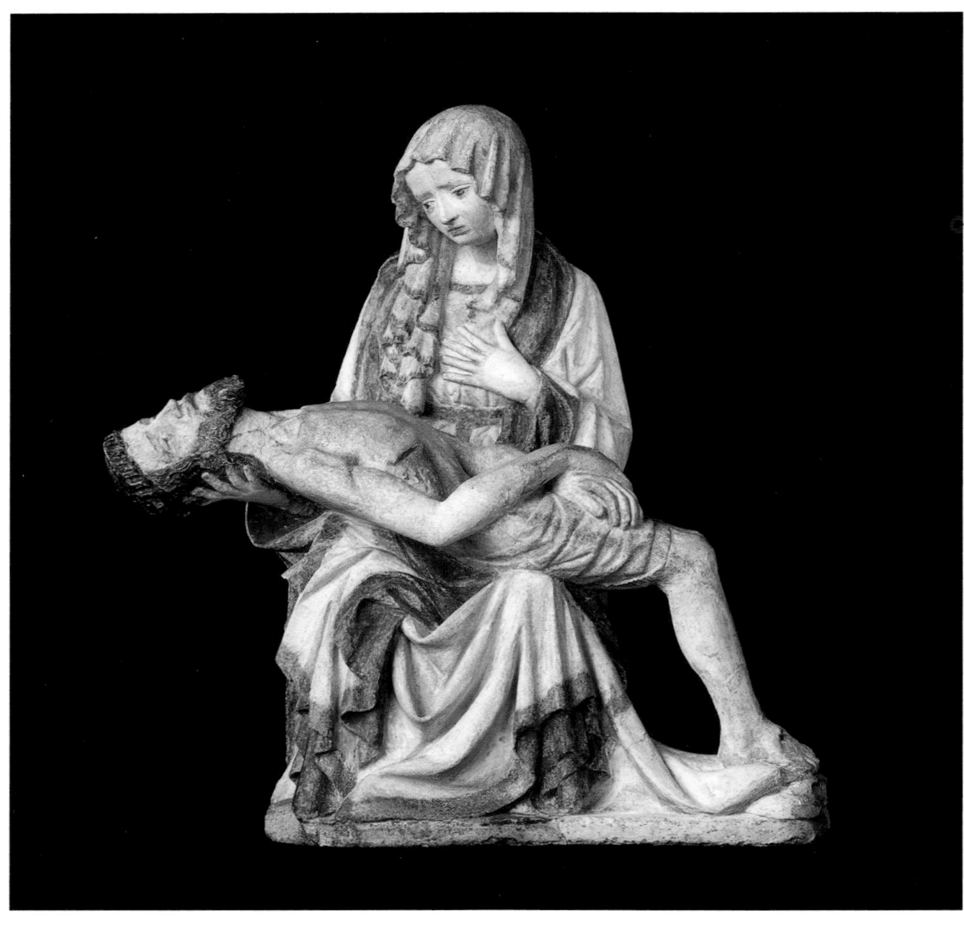

WESTERN PRUSSIA

Circa 1400

Opening Madonna

Polychrome wood
(limewood)
H. 0.20 m; W. 0.45 m (open)
Acquired 1890
Cl. 12060

The simple forms of this Madonna and Child encompass a complex iconography. Divided in the middle, the Virgins' body opens to display inside two typical late-medieval representations. The inner sides of the wings show the Madonna of Mercy, spreading her ample cloak over the faithful; in the center, the Trinity is featured in the form of the Throne of Grace: God the Father holding the Crucified Christ (replaced here by an eighteenth-century ivory Christ), accompanied by the dove of the Holy Ghost (lost).

The creation of this new marial iconography should be attributed to the Teutonic order, placed under the Virgin's protection. The profound meaning of this group can be deciphered in the writings of a contemporary theologian, Johannes Marienwerder (1343-1417), who mentioned the triple birth of Jesus: by the Father without the Mother (the Throne of Grace), by the Mother without the Father (Madonna and Child), and within men's hearts (the Madonna of Mercy). However, these representations were condemned by the Church and became increasingly rare during the fifteenth century.

E. A.

Madonna and Child, reliquary of the umbilicus of Christ

Gilded silver, colored glass
H. 0.33 m; W. 0.19 m;
D. 0.17 m
Kept at Notre-Dame-en-Vaux (Châlons-sur-Marne) until 1727; purchased by François Clément; Soltykoff collection; acquired 1861
Cl. 3307

The story of this lovely Madonna and Child is well-known. It was made in 1407 through the good offices of the testamentary executors of Thibault des Abbés, a bourgeois from Châlons-sur-Marne, and contained the only relic of the Holy Navel conserved in France (the inner case of the reliquary is a modern restoration).

This accurately dated work highlights a remarkable stage in French art around 1400. Stylistically we can attribute it either to a Parisian goldsmith or to a Paris-trained goldsmith from Champagne. The highly plastic character of the group, the sweetness of the expression combined with the fluidity and elegance of the drapery make this reliquary a match for the loveliest jewels crafted at the time in the Parisian capital for a princely clientele.

E. A.

PARIS

Circa 1410-1420

God the Father flanked by the four Evangelists

Miniature on vellum

H. 0.36 m; W. 0.26 m

Anonymous donation, 1885

Cl. 11315

At the turn of the century, Paris was a lively center of illuminated book production, which had begun to appeal to aristocratic society and the wealthy bourgeoisie. From an illustrious Parisian family—the Montaigus—known for their taste and manuscripts collection, the museum boasts two leaves from a breviary. The Crucifixion bears the arms of Gérard de Montaigu, who was bishop of Paris in 1409 and chancellor to the Duke of Berry, another great art connoisseur.

On the leaf shown here, the image of God the Father, an elongated, flowing figure enthroned amidst the four evangelists, is typical of the international Gothic. However, under the influence of the Master of Boucicaut, the prevailing taste in Paris in the early fifteenth century reflected the attempt to represent space: the four Evangelists, John (and the eagle), Luke (and the bull), Matthew (and the angel) and Mark (and the lion), are seated at their desks against a three-dimensional background, after models from the workshop of the Master of Rohan, another of the capital's great miniaturists.

S. L.

Before 1457

Tarascon Pietà

Paint on wood
H. 0.84 m; W. 1.30 m
From the castle of Tarascon (Vaucluse); Louvre deposit, 1910
Cl. 18509

For the year 1457, the inventory of the castle of Tarascon mentions a "new" altarpiece "of Our Lord in Our Lady's arms", placed "in the queen's new room", that of Jeanne de Laval, the wife of king René. Purchased from the Tarascon hospice, the painting represents the theme of the *Pietà*. Christ taken from the Cross is held by His mother, surrounded by Saint John and three Holy Women, including Mary Magdalene, depicted with her attribute, the perfume vase. The panel's theme as well as its dramatic rendering and deeply folded drapery derives from the Flemish painter Rogier Van der Weyden (1399 or 1400-1464). Provençal, the artist was also familiar with the Avignon *Pietà* (Louvre) painted by Enguerrand Quarton (active between1444 and 1466) from whom he borrowed the frieze-like composition of the figures that appear here on a golden ground. It has been suggested that the panel could be by a Dombet, whose family was known in Aix in the mid-fifteenth century for its painting on glass.

S. L.

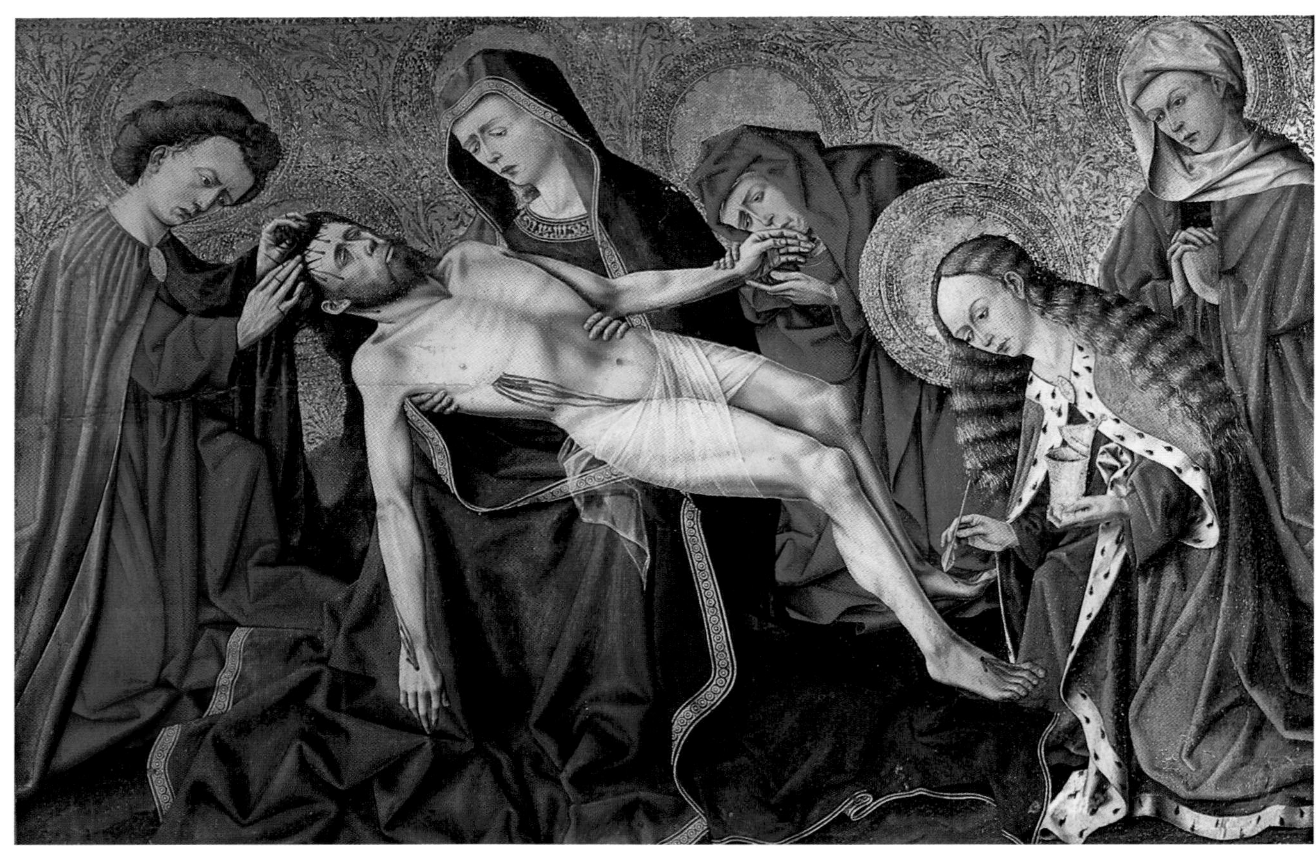

Circa 1460

Rondel with the monogramme LG

Transparent glass, grisaille,
silver stain, lead
Diam. 0.195 m
Du Sommerard collection
Cl. 1037 a

Roundels, small medallions made of a single piece of glass painted in grisaille and (the french says yellow silver) silver stain that gives them this precious golden color, adorned civil windows in the late Middle Ages. The LG roundel is one of the oldest secular roundels extant. The letters have been identified as the initials of Laurent Gyrard, secretary and notary to the king, inspector of taxes for the Languedoil from 1452 to 1486. The author may be Jean Fouquet, one of the greatest French painters of that time, or a very close collaborator of his. The maidens recall the shield-bearers of the Simon de Varie's Book of Hours, signed by Fouquet. The delicacy of the motifs and the style, the turbaned heads, blond, curly locks of hair, and gentle melancholy of the eyes belong to his repertory, whereas the technique, in particular the folds hollowed by stippled matt shading, suggests a miniaturist's hand.

S. L.

Dijon
Second quarter of the XVth century

Madonna and Child

Limestone
H. 0.97 m
Possibly from the portal of the castle of Saint-Apollinaire, near Dijon; Timbal bequest, 1881
Cl. 18926

In the fifteenth century, the States of Burgundy were among the most powerful in the western world, and their wealth nurtured art patronage. Philip the Bold attracted several of the greatest artists to the building site of the Champmol Charterhouse, the dukes' burial ground by the gates of Dijon. One of them, the sculptor Claus Sluter, inspired fifteenth-century sculpture by giving up the refined elegance of the fourteenth-century image-carvers in favor of greater expressiveness.

This Madonna and Child from the vicinity of Dijon is characteristic of Sluter's influence on Burgundian sculpture, the minute features of the Virgin's face contrast with her off-balanced silhouette and ample, expressive volumes, outlined by the heavy drapery of her veil and cloak.

E. A.

NOTTINGHAM OR YORK

Circa 1400

The Resurrection of Christ

Polychrome alabaster
H. 0.40 m; W. 0.27 m;
D. 0.06 m
Sauvageot donation
1856
Cl. 19328

The Midlands, in the center of England, has a great many alabaster quarries that for two centuries, from the mid-fourteenth century until the Anglican Reformation, around 1550, furnished countless sculpture workshops. The main centers were York and Nottingham, where they produced statues but mainly altarpiece panels that were sent beyond England to all over Europe.

The museum possesses an important collection of these altarpiece panels enlivened by extremely bright polychromy. Most of them were dedicated to the life of Christ or the life of the Virgin, which lead to standard, occasionally repetitive, production. This Resurrection scene, of a relatively early date, avoids these weaknesses by contrasting the vigor and majesty of Christ risen from the grave with the languid sleeping soldiers.

E. A.

Circa 1483

Passion altarpiece

Polychrome wood
H. 0.97 m; W. 0.90 m (open);
D. 0.21 m
Debruge-Duménil collection; Soltykoff collection; acquired 1861
Cl. 3269

The last centuries of the Middle Ages, in the field of Germanic sculpture, were truly a golden age. Altarpieces, produced in large quantities, usually combined carving in the central panel and painting on the wings. This Passion altarpiece, in a remarkable state of conservation, is a perfect illustration of the utter virtuosity displayed by artists working on a small altarpiece intended for private devotion.

The Nativity and the Adoration of the Magi are painted on the outside of the wings, while the six panels inside recall the Passion of Christ. In the center, the carved figures theatrically enact the Mourning scene: in front of the Calvary, a group of people in dramatic postures surround Christ's rigid body deposed from the Cross and offered to meditation; as the Virgin holds her son on her lap, Saint John and the Holy Women express their grief by their gestures and expressions. To the right, a praying Carthusian monk is presented by his patron saint, Saint Andrew. The presence of this donor, as well as the cityscape in the background of the Adoration of the Magi have led scholars to attribute the commission of the altarpiece to a Carthusian of the Kranenburg house, near Nimwegen.

The altarpiece has kept its original, highly refined polychromy: on the inner side of the panel, a punched foliage decoration enhances the gold ground; and the figures' apparel is heightened by applied brocades that emulate precious fabrics. The Holy Women, in particular Mary Magdalene who holds her perfume vase, are also richly clothed; the delicacy of their countenances, the elegance of their attire and of their gestures qualify them as masterpieces of Medieval sculpture.

The treatment of the drapery, with its sharp, angular folds, along with the emphasis placed on the pathetic character of the scene attest the influence of Rogier Van der Weyden (1399 or 1400-1464) on sculptors of the Lowlands and the Rhineland. The style of the carvings, with its tremulous sensitivity, belongs to a famous artist from Kalkar, master Arnt, whose active workshop executed the stalls of the Minorities church at Cleves, the Saint George altarpiece for the church of Saint-Nicholas of Kalkar, as well as countless other works.

E. A.

The Lady with the Unicorn: Hearing

Wool, silk
H. 3.68 m; W. 2.90 m
Castle of Boussac (Creuse);
acquired 1882
Cl. 10833

The wall hanging of the *Lady with the Unicorn* is rightfully famous. Discovered in 1841 in the castle of Boussac, its luminosity, mystery, and poetry continue to dazzle visitors. Composed of six tapestries on a bright red ground constellated with "millefleurs", the wall hanging illustrates the five senses. The widely-repeated coat-of-arms, borne by two heraldic animals of the medieval bestiary, the lion and the unicorn, identifies the patron as Jean le Viste (died in 1500). This gentleman of the robe from Lyons attained the height of honors, when he became counsellor to the king, benefitting from nobiliary privileges. In all likelihood a Parisian painter designed the cartoons of this rare iconography and Brussels workshops wove it in wool and silk threads. In the tapestry of *Hearing*, the Lady is playing a portable organ set upon a table covered with a rich carpet, while her maid servant is pumping the bellows. The "millefleurs" background swarms with birds and familiar animals (fox, lamb, rabbit) or exotic ones (leopard, lion, monkey). The flowers planted on the dark blue island serving as the ground in the scene add a touch of realism that contrasts with the preciousness of the figures.

V. H.

The Lady with the Unicorn: « À mon seul désir »

Wool, silk
H. 3.77 m; W. 4.73 m
Castle of Boussac (Creuse);
acquired 1882
Cl. 10834

In the sixth tapestry of the wall hanging, the Lady, beautifully dressed, is putting her jewelry back in the casket her maid servant is holding out to her. The scene is set in front of a tent made of rich embroidered velvet upheld on each side by the two heraldic animals—lion and unicorn—bearing the motto "*À mon seul désir*" ("To my own desire"). The scholarly iconography opposes the pleasures of the senses illustrated in the five other tapestries to the asceticism of the spirit. The final allegory relates to the sixth sense that philosophers and theologians of the early Renaissance spoke of, the sense of understanding, of the heart. The scene, with its lovely composition, combines the various elements, playing admirably with contrasting colors and the heraldic and decorative repertory. The youthful Lady's elegance blends gracefully and poetically with the small animals and the "millefleurs".

V. H.

BRUSSELS
Circa 1490-1500

Saint Mary Magdalene

Wood (oak), formerly polychrome
H. 0.97 m; W. 0.36 m; D. 0.24 m
Debruge-Duménil collection; acquired 1850
Cl. 1851

Mary Magdalene was a highly popular saint in the late Middle Ages; tradition assembled in a single person three women mentioned in the Gospels: the sinner who attended the meal at Simon's house, pouring a vase of perfume over Christ's feet, Mary of Bethany, the sister of Martha and Lazarus and model of the contemplative life, and Mary of Magdala, one of the Holy Women who had followed Christ to the Crucifixion and came to the grave to embalm Him.

On this splendid sculpture from Brussels the saint holds her attribute, the perfume vase. She is depicted as a young woman with a lovely face and a sophisticated hairstyle, with braids wound around and crossed over her bonnet. In the late Middle Ages, devotional statuary is often adorned with an entirely secular elegance.

E. A.

Circa 1515-1520

Altarpiece of the Passion and the Childhood of Christ

Polychrome wood (oak)
H. 2.90 m; W. 2.58 m;
D. 0.34 m
From the storerooms of Saint-Denis; entered the museum in 1889
Cl. 11923

In the late fifteenth and early sixteenth century, the production of large carved and painted altarpieces was growing considerably in Antwerp, an international commercial hub. Antwerp altarpieces, exported all over Europe, are identifiable by the marks the guild of Saint-Luke put on them: a cut hand guaranteed the quality of the wood and two cut hands topped by a castle guaranteed the polychromy. The popularity of these altarpieces can be explained by their relatively modest cost, as well as by the simplicity of their iconographic content, for the most part illustrating scenes from the Childhood and the Passion of Christ. The museum's altarpiece is characterized by its narrative mood, enlivened by a swarming throng of figures with heightened expressions. The women's extraordinary hairstyles, the rich brocades of their garments, the elaborate, and unusual armors of the soldiers could but attract the eyes of the faithful, enchant them and lead them to the contemplation of sacred history.

E. A.

Brussels
Circa 1500

Tapestry of the life of Saint Stephen: the Miracle of the mules

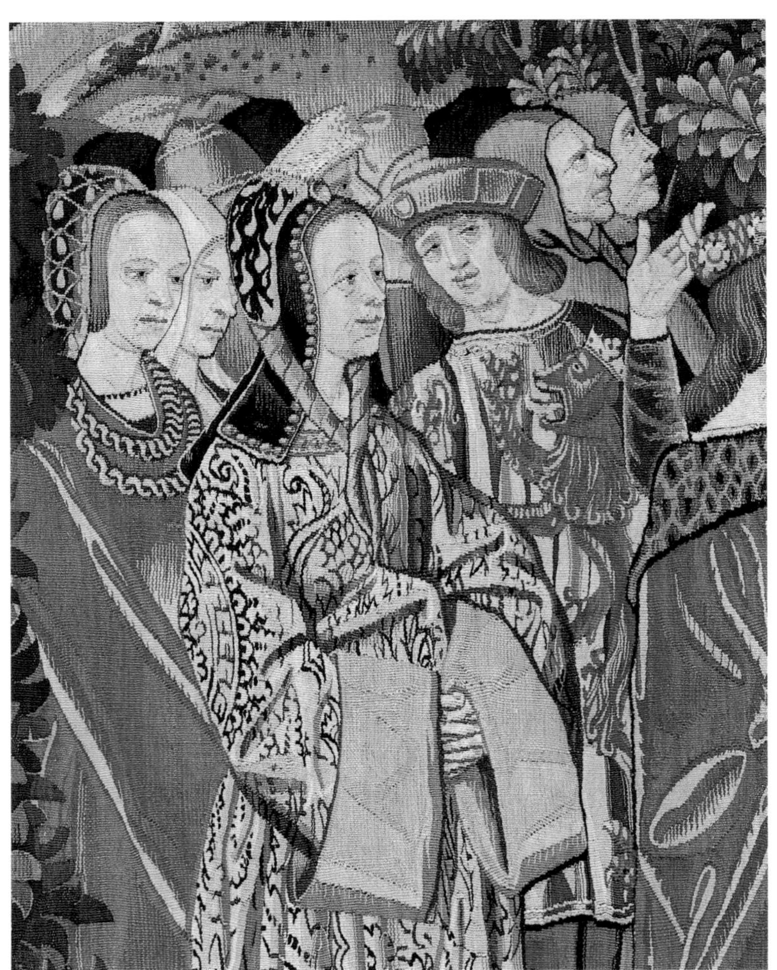

Offered by the bishop of Auxerre, Jean Baillet (1472-1503), and hung in the choir of his cathedral, this series of tapestries illustrate, like one of our contemporary comic strips, the life of the patron saint of the church. 45 meters long for a height of 1,70 meters, the wall-hanging, fortunately complete, features twelve pieces woven in wool and silk threads. Each of the images is commented on a cartouche in French, whereas the dialogues between the actors are woven in Latin inside the scenes. The iconography is inspired by the Acts of the Apostles, but mainly by the *Golden Legend*. It carefully describes the miracles that took place after the discovery of the remains of the first martyr of the Church and the events surrounding the arrival of his reliquary in Rome. The scene shows the mules' refusal to carry the reliquary to the Emperor of Constantinople, since this was not God's will. The rather fine weaving is typical of the Brussels workshops. Likewise, some details of the composition—the realism of the poses, the wealth of the rendering of the garments—attribute the cartoons to a Brussels painter, Colyn de Coter (1450-1539). Miraculously preserved during the Revolution in the attics of Auxerre Hospice, the wall hanging was purchased by the museum in 1880 and is one of its textile masterpieces.

V. H.

Wool, silk
H. 1.66 m; W. 3.96 m
Cathedral of Auxerre (Yonne); acquired 1880
Cl. 9935

Choir Stalls from Saint-Lucien of Beauvais

Oak
H. 0.87 m
Storerooms of Saint-Denis; entered the museum in 1889-1890
Cl. 19603-19682

Well-known from the time it was completed, this ensemble is all the more valuable because it testifies to the patronage of the abbot Antoine Du Bois (1492-1507), and is carved in the lively style that characterized Picardy workshops at that time.

Here, the constitutive sculpted elements (sides, seat framings and misericords) depict Saint Peter entrusting the evangelization of the Beauvaisis to Lucian and his two companions, alongside fantastic animals and hybrid creatures, two acrobats, and a man rolling a globe of the earth in front of him.

A second narrative cycle relates several episodes of the life of Saint Anthony, the commissioner's patron saint. As for the other misericords, they display religious and secular scenes in an order that we are no longer able to grasp, but which expresses the fear of the devil and hell that characterized the late Middle Ages.

J. F.

ITALY (velvet) / FLANDERS (orphrey)

XVth century

The Tree of Jesse

Chasuble
Silk, gold threads
H. 1.205 m; W. 0.64 m
donated by Guy Ladrière,
1986
Cl. 23269

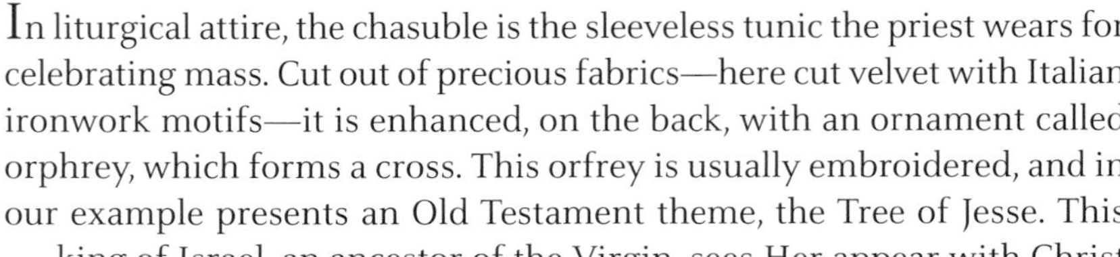

In liturgical attire, the chasuble is the sleeveless tunic the priest wears for celebrating mass. Cut out of precious fabrics—here cut velvet with Italian ironwork motifs—it is enhanced, on the back, with an ornament called orphrey, which forms a cross. This orfrey is usually embroidered, and in our example presents an Old Testament theme, the Tree of Jesse. This king of Israel, an ancestor of the Virgin, sees Her appear with Christ amidst his descent. The rich embroidery work, exemplary of late Middle-Age Flemish workshops, associates the ground silk threads on a taffeta base worked and couched with the figures embroidered in split stitches.

V. H.

SOUTH LOWLANDS

Early XVIth century

The Grape Harvest

Wool, silk

H. 2.46 m; W. 4.95 m

Dolfuss bequest, 1930

Cl. 21541

The left side, on a conventional "millefleurs" ground, illustrates the pressing of the grapes, either in the vat or with the hand press, under the supervision of a patrician couple; the right side shows the harvesting of the grapes in a natural setting, with a scene of budding gallantry. This everyday-life theme is part of a wall hanging of which several woven pieces are dispersed throughout the world, in particular *Picking the Grapes.* The origin of the models should be sought in France, where books printed in the capital reproduce similar figures. Skillfully joined up in the middle, the two fragments of tapestry were fine-drawn at the time of the weaving of the coats-of-arms, which, unfortunately, is undecipherable in the upper corners. Because of the style of the costumes, we cannot date the execution of the tapestry farther back than the early sixteenth century. The vividness of the colors and the picturesque composition give this piece its special charm.

V. H.

F R A N C E

Circa 1480-1500

Folding table

Oak

H. 0.75 m; W. 0.90 m;

L. 0.79 m

Gastaud donation, 1959

Cl. 22795

Probably unique of its kind, this table, held together by tenons, mortises, and pegs, can be entirely taken apart and transported easily, in keeping with the customs of the Middle Ages. Featuring an octagonal top, it was eventually placed in the chamber. This kind of furniture, mentioned in texts as early as the fourteenth century, was especially widespread in German countries where, when it was enhanced with marquetry, it could also be used as a game table.

Whereas the human figures that form the extremities of the base can no longer be identified, the feet panels slide in runners carved in the legs decorated with foliage and scale motifs, and are ornamented with delicate flamboyant tracery that dates this table to the late fifteenth century.

J. F.

SPANISH LEVANT (MANISSES OR PATERNA)

Circa 1465

Vase with Winged Handles

Lusterware

H. 0.60 m; Diam. 0.226 m

Ricci collection; acquired 1862

Cl. 7647

The technique of lusterware appeared in Iraq in the ninth century and was practiced in Islamic Spain by the thirteenth century. A little before 1400, Morisco artists, Muslims living in Christian countries, brought the technique to the Valencia region, developing a production that would be exported all over Europe, especially to Italy where, under the name "majolica", it was so widely emulated that it gave rise to the Italian faience production. This large vase with wing handles is outstanding in the museum collections. While its decorative blue and golden ivy leaves can be found on numerous works of the third quarter of the fifteenth century, its dimensions and majestic shape are exceptional. When compared with a similar vase bearing the Medici arms kept in the British Museum (Godman 619), the date of this work appears to be around 1465.

X. D.

S o u t h   L o w l a n d s

First quarter of the XVIth century

La Vie Seigneuriale (The Lord's Life): The Bath

Wool, silk
H. 2.85 m; W. 2.85 m
Acquired 1852
Cl. 2180

In 1852, Edmond Du Sommerard purchased six tapestries from an aristocratic Rouen family illustrating the life of a nobleman and his wife around 1500. Woven with wool thread, the series is a "millefleurs" characteristic of Brabant workshops. Amidst a profusion of plants, the luxuriously attired figures look as if they had been poised there without having anything to do with one another. The custom of tapestry craftsmen to reuse cartoons explains the stiff appearance of the weaving. Thus the figure of the servant of the *Bath* can be seen again with a different hairstyle and dress on the next tapestry, *The Promenade*. On a background of planted flowers, a nude young woman is immersed in a tub adorned with acanthus and lion muzzles recalling the art of the Renaissance. The hairstyles and the heavy, angular folds of the garments attest to models from the Southern Lowlands.

V. H.

France (?)

Late XVth century

Game box

Ebony, stained walnut, ivory

H. 0.39 m; W. 0.24 m (closed)

Acquired 1862

Cl. 3434

A quality object crafted with care, this game box is one of the oldest known in French public collections. It is also a rarity due to the number of games it contains. We can discover a tourniquet—also known as needle roulette—a game of fox and geese, a game of merils, a chessboard, a backgammon, and, on the outside, a game of *glic*. The latter, a card game usually for three players, is often mentioned as early as the 1450's.

In the fifteenth century, the technique of ivory inlay was practiced mainly in Italy, and in particular in Venice, but the presence of Italian ivory workers active in France during this period might confirm that we indeed have here a "French make", as it figures in the inventory of the museum's collections.

J. F.

Bibliography

Visit Guides

ADAM (Jean-Pierre) and DELHUMEAU (Herveline), *Les Thermes antiques de Lutèce*, Paris, Réunion des musées nationaux, 1996 (2nd ed. 2001).

ANTOINE (Élisabeth), *Musée national du Moyen Âge – Thermes de Cluny. Le tour du musée en 80 œuvres*, Paris, Réunion des musées nationaux, 1995.

ANTOINE (Élisabeth), *Le Jardin médiéval*, Paris, Réunion des musées nationaux, 2000.

ERLANDE-BRANDENBURG (Alain), *Les Statues de Notre-Dame de Paris*, Paris, Réunion des musées nationaux, 1986 (2nd ed. 1994).

ERLANDE-BRANDENBURG (Alain), LE POGAM (Pierre-Yves) and SANDRON (Dany), *Musée national du Moyen Âge – Thermes de Cluny. Guide to the collections*, Paris, Réunion des musées nationaux, 1993 (English ed.).

LE POGAM (Pierre-Yves), *Musée national du Moyen Âge – Thermes de Cluny*, Paris, Réunion des musées nationaux, 1994.

TABURET-DELAHAYE (Élisabeth), *Les Ivoires du musée de Cluny*, Paris, Réunion des musées nationaux, 1981 (2nd ed. 1988).

Catalogues raisonnes

BRUNA (Denis), *Enseignes de pèlerinage et enseignes profanes au musée national du Moyen Âge*, Paris, Réunion des musées nationaux, 1996.

CAILLET (Jean-Pierre), *L'Antiquité classique, le Haut Moyen Âge et Byzance au musée de Cluny : sculpture et décoration monumentale*, Paris, Réunion des musées nationaux, 1985.

DESROSIERS (Sophie), *Soieries et autres textiles de l'Antiquité au XVIe siècle – Musée national du Moyen Âge – Thermes de Cluny*, Paris, Réunion des musées nationaux (forthcoming in 2003).

HUCHARD (Viviane), *The Musée national du Moyen Âge – Thermes de Cluny*, Paris, Réunion des musées nationaux, 1996 (English ed.).

JOUBERT (Fabienne), *La Tapisserie médiévale au musée de Cluny*, Paris, Réunion des musées nationaux, 1987 (2nd ed. 2002).

LORQUIN (Alexandra), *Les Tissus coptes du musée national du Moyen Âge – Thermes de Cluny. Étoffes de lin et de laine*, Paris, Réunion des musées nationaux, 1992.

PRIGENT (Christiane), *Les Sculptures anglaises d'albâtre au musée national du Moyen Âge – Thermes de Cluny*, Paris, Réunion des musées nationaux, 1998.

TABURET-DELAHAYE (Élisabeth), *L'Orfèvrerie gothique (XIIIe-début XVe siècle) au musée de Cluny*, Paris, Réunion des musées nationaux, 1989.

Photography credits

© CRRMF: p. 23. © Fondation BNP-Paribas, Hugo Maertens: cover (right), p. 12, 15, 17, 21, 25, 27, 29, 32, 34,44, 45, 59, 60, 65, 71, 74, 76, 79, 86, 98, 103, 105, 106, 108, 110, 112, 117. © Réunion des musées nationaux, Paris: p. 32, 33, 36, 37, 39, 46, 47, 54 (right), 83, 85, 88, 96, 102; photo Arnaudet: p. 6-7, 8, 11; photo Berizzi: cover (right), p. 20, 48, 49, 51, 118 (above and below), 121, backcover; photo Blot: couverture (left), p. 22, 28, 31, 38, 40, 41, 42, 43, 47 (left), 52, 57, 58, 61, 63, 64, 66 (left and right), 69, 78, 82, 87 (right), 89, 93, 97 (above and below), 107, 111, 113, 116, 120, 122, 123; photo Gaspari: p. 114, 115; photo Lewandowski: p. 23, 56, 99, 109, 119, 125; photo Ojeda: p. 80, 81, 84, 87 (left); photo Thierry Ollivier: back cover (background); photo Raux: p. 50, 53, 55, 62, 67, 73, 75, 77, 91, 92, 95, 100, 101, 104, 124. Right reserved: p. 13, 18.

Produced by the Publishing division under the direction of Béatrice Foulon

Editorial coordination:
Geneviève Rudolf

Translation:
Susan Wise

Adaptation and copy editing:
Marie Aquilino and Julia Fritsch

Illustrations:
Herveline Pousse, Agence photographique de la Réunion des Musées Nationaux

Documentation:
Musée national du Moyen Age documentation service

Cover design:
Gilles Huot / HDL Design

Graphic design and layout:
Cécile Neuville

Production:
Philippe Gournay

Photoengraving by Bussière, Paris

The book was printed and manufactured at the Kapp Lahure Jombart press in Évreux

Acknowledgments:
The Réunion des Musées Nationaux and the Musée national du Moyen Age owe a debt of gratitude to the Fondation BNP-Paribas (Mr. Jean-Jacques Goron) for its contribution to this publication.

Legal deposit : Septembre 2003
ISBN: 2-7118-4644-X
RMN : GA 20 46 44

Printed in France